Sandra ON THE ROCKS

VOLUME 1
OMNIBUS

STORY
David Lumsdon

ART & LETTERING
Saiful Remy "Eisu" Mokhtar

SERIES EDITOR
T Campbell

Follow us online at:
sandraontherocks.com

THANK YOUS

Big thanks to my Mom, Eisu, T, Gisèle, and an extra big thanks to every last one of you readers; you guys are awesome!
Love, David :)

Thanks to Dave, T, and Gisèle for all their help and support in the making of this series, and thanks to all my fans and readers for supporting me and believing in me. Thank you!
Love, Eisu

CONTENTS

CHAPTER 1
Freckles Among the Stars 7

CHAPTER 2
Mancake and Carrot Cake 20

CHAPTER 3
Karma Chamelia 35

CHAPTER 4
Geek Chic U 65

CHAPTER 5
Girls' Night Out 115

BONUS STORY
Twisted Tuesday 162

CHAPTER 6
Baking with Fury 169

CHAPTER 7
Pumped 189

CHAPTER 8
Shower Thoughts 199

CHAPTER 9
The Gamer Trio 214

BONUS STORY
Sweet Dreams 260

FOREWORD

When I was asked to do an intro regarding why we chose Sandra, our plucky binge drinker with a penchant for kink under the influence, to be the star of her own series I immediately thought, "Hmm... that's a good question... so much has happened that it all seems like a bit of a blur now."

So let's start at the beginning, shall we? First and foremost, we needed to get rid of Sandra from "MÉNAGE À 3". Nothing permanent mind you, we had just culminated our story arc of Sandra's awkward date with DiDi and needed to give DiDi a little breathing room as to what should happen to her next. That's where the idea for pairing Sandra up with the ever-glamorous Senna came up, we figured we'd give Sandra some globe-hopping adventures in the background of MA3 with Senna as her comic foil until we were ready to re-integrate her into Montreal.

We approached Eisu who had done a guest strip for us to do a short story that ran in MA3. It later became the original "Sandra on the Rocks" strips where Sandra emancipates herself from Senna and begins her fledgling career as a model. Honestly, I couldn't have asked for a better artist to bring this world to life. Eisu truly made SOTR look fun and distinct.

I'm not sure whose idea it was to continue these strips into a full-fledged spinoff but we were spinning off our various webcomics like crazy at the time. At our height I was writing/co-writing five series at once. Looking back at it now I'm not sure how I kept all the characters straight.

It was Cassandra Wedeking, our collaborator on DANGEROUSLY CHLOE, that came up with the title "SANDRA ON THE ROCKS". She was always good at coming up with clever titles. Once we had the title, I then had to go about crafting Sandra's world. I didn't have much of a series plan at the beginning and was making it up as we went along.

Thinking about it, it's almost scary how some characters started out quite differently than what we ended up with. Zoé, Sandra's mother figure and mentor was originally going to be one of Domenico's assistants. It was a last-minute change that made her into the "veteran model" and every bit Domenico's equal. SOTR would have turned out very differently without Zoé there to both guide Sandra and give her an ideal to shoot for, not that Sandra appreciated it, she fought Zoé every inch of the way.

Another last-minute change was Sandra's BFF "Lavali". In the script Lavali was described of being of Indian descent, but when Eisu turned in the page he drew her with such a stern expression that it didn't suit the more "fun" person she was supposed to be. After a quick deliberation we decided to swap her out with the Dark Matter Games employee we saw shoving Sandra away in the "Mimzy Molar" costume before returning as "Carmen Chamelia". After the strip went up, the realization slowly dawned on us that...

"Lavali still has her Indian name..."

"Oh..."

"Ohhhh......"

"..."

"Wh-whatever, we'll just explain that her parents were hippies or something later."

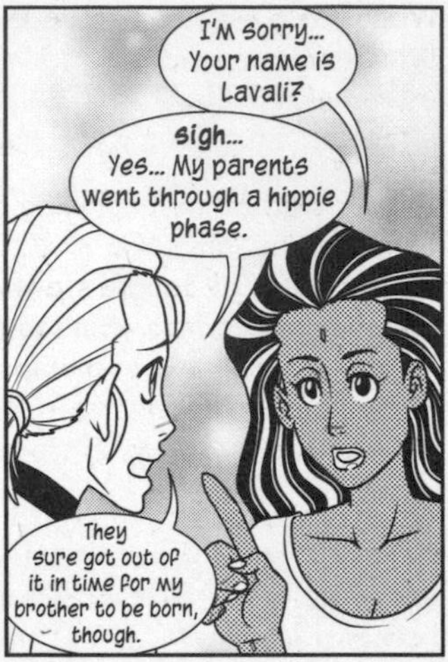

Fun fact: Eisu reused Lavali's original design as Simone, the trendy fashion boutique owner.

When we started the series, my intent was to write a series that would please a more female audience. You can see a bit of that through Sandra's early relationship with the hunky baker Pierre. I feel I stayed on point with that for the first book but then fell into my trappings of "everyone's a lesbian" in vol 2 lol. Sandra's romance with Pierre really got neglected in later volumes, I guess Sandra's career just took precedence.

My one regret was that we never got to do the planned "Sandra on the Rocks: Rock Bottom" story arc. Had there been another book, the last story would have ended on a darker note... and I mean daaaaaaaaark... like, "we'll-probably-loose-half-our-readership-over-this-but-lets-do-it-anyway" dark. Through a series of drunken mistakes and meddling from Eloise, Sandra would have ended up alienating everyone in her life and destroying her fledgling career with Eloise taking her spot as Zoé's protégé and Pierre's lover. Without a friend in the world the last story would have ended with Sandra's "apparent" suicide. To really commit to the bit we would have changed the banner on the SOTR site to read "Eloise Rocks" for the first little bit which would have started with various characters reacting to Sandra having vanished from her lives. I even planned to go as far as to have Tatiana going to the morgue to identify a body that would have turned out not to be Sandra. And until Sandra's return there would not have been a single joke, I wanted it to be as gut-wrenching as possible. The rest of the book would have been Sandra returning, gaining the trust of all her friends back and clawing her way back out of the ashes of her career like a phoenix, thus ending the series on a high note.

In the end we did do a smaller version of "Rock Bottom" near the end of the series though it was decidedly more lighthearted.

Alas, all good things had to end. Thinking of all the series I worked on, ending SOTR was the one I had the hardest time letting go. I really think we created something special here, with fun endearing characters that part of me hopes we can revisit someday. One of my favorites that never got enough screen time was the constant thorn in Sandra's side, Tatiana. I really liked that besides being all business she still has a soft spot for her tablet "Yulia".

I hope you all enjoy reading SANDRA ON THE ROCKS as much as I did writing it.

Cheers!

~DAVE

Freckles Among the Stars

Oh, wow, a photo shoot! In Brazil! This model assistant thing is gonna be so much fun, Senna!
I can't wait to tell my friends in Montreal!
They're gonna be jealousss! It's SO glamorous, am I right?!
Sandra, when I'm around, everything is glamorous.
So... how do I assist?
You can start by running to the nearest shop and fetching me a drink.
A glamorous drink?
No, a Guaraná Antarctica will do nicely.
Are you sure you don't want anything else...?
S-Something with... fewer *vowels?*

Sennaaaaa! I got your drink!
Great! Bring it out to me.
I... I don't have any swimwear!
But I'm thirsty nowwwwww!
Ow! Pebble!
Ew! Seaweed!
EEK! TINY FISHES! Whoa! Whoa! Wh--
SPLASH!!
Guaraná Kuat? Blech! Wrong brand! Take it back!

That's Guaraná Antarctica, I wanted Guaraná Antarctica *Ice!*
No you didn't!
Well, I do now!
I said Guaraná Antarctica Ice! This is Guaraná Antarctica *Zero!* Good for my figure, but I dislike the aftertaste!
Guaraná Antarctica Açai?! That's an *energy drink*, dummy!
Never mind, I think I'll just have the regular Guaraná Antarctica after all.
Good, I left the can in a cool--
Oh, make sure it's in a glass bottle! Tastes more authentic!

Monday: Highlight interesting passages from Senna's Diaries for potential future biography.
Wednesday: Cook Senna gourmet meal for romantic dinner with Miguel.
Saturday: Distract a male model's jealous groupie while Senna has a private discussion with him. Later learn that "groupie" is actually male model's fiancée. Keep story out of newspapers.

Worst. Job. Ever!
Woo-hoo! Best job ever!

<Senna! Senna!>
<Not now, Celina, I am having my makeup done!>
<There has been a change in photographers! >
<For this you bother me?>
<It's Domenico Pedrazzini!>
<No way! He's way too rich and famous to be doing THIS shoot!>
<He is, he is! And have you seen the pictures of his chest? SPICY!>
<Celina, don't be naïve. Those pictures are Photoshopped.>
Ciao, ragazze! Talking time is over! Picture time is now!
KYAAAAA!
<I have never been happier to be wrong!>

It is such an honor to be working with you!
Bella, please! You are, how you say, correct!
=HUFF HUFF= Senna!
=HUFF= Here's your Sal... Sap... Salip... fancy salad I can't pronounce!
Ah, yes, my Salpicao De Galinha! Is it from the right caterer this time?
Yes! The caterer that's on the other end of town, for which I had to get up at the crack of dawn to walk there and back here before lunch!
Well, I'm not very hungry today. Just put it in the fridge for tomorrow.
That's... it! That's it!
I AM GOING TO KILL--
YMFFFFF....
You! Ragazza! What is wrong with your face?
She grimaces like that every day. I think she's allergic to work.

This one has freckles! Models do not have freckles!
Whaff going onff?
You! You do not have "the freckles!"
Of course not! I have perfect complexion!
Well, maybe you *should* have freckles! Have you ever thought of that?
I have decided! Send this girl to wardrobe! She will be in the shoot!
What?!
I will show the world the beauty of her freckles!
???

Wait! There must be some mistake!
Indeed! She is no model! She is my assistant!
Is what she says true? You are her lowly assistant?
I don't know 'bout lowly... b-but yes.
And you have no modeling experience whatsoever?
N-Not as such, no.
Then you are my discovery! Domenico will guide you, mold you, make you something more than human!
...
....

You're out on a night on the town! You want to have fun! Is that your lover? Nooo! It's his brother, Enriqué!
...
Now you are at the club! You are dancing! Where is that waiter with your drink?
He's with his lover, Raoul, in the broom closet!
Yes! Yes! You are an angel! A naughty angel in lingerie! Show me what heaven is like!
That's it! You are wearing the swimsuit your father forbade you to wear!
There's that boy from math class you like! Impress him!

Whew! And I thought being your assistant was exhausting!
Humph!
Hey, don't be like that! You'll get plenty of shots too!
Not with you getting all his attention!
Ah, Senna, there you are! I have *perfect shot* for you together with Sandra!
Really?
Now's my chance to upstage her!
Yes! Yes! That's the way! Growl like you mean it!
Grrrr!

Ha-ha-ha! These will come out *perfect!* You are my muse, freckled one!
Umm... *good!* That's good. Right?
You will follow me for more shoots during my stay in Brazil. Then, you will come with me to Paris, Munich, Milan, Hong Kong, and Tokyo; where I will make you a *STAR!*
A stuh-- not *meeee!* I'm too *plain!*
Ha-ha! *Modesty!* This will go away!
D'you hear that? I'm a muse! And a star! And... MODEST!
So that's it? You're just leaving? What about *me?!*
Well, I guess... I could use an assistant!

Mancake and Carrot Cake

Dear Desirée,
Can you believe it?
I'm in Paris!
I'm going to stay at Domenico's penthouse where I'll learn how to be a model.
Arrival
SANDRA ARDEN
Gotta run, I have plenty more e-mails to send.
Hugs & kisses,
Sandra
Dear Senna,
HA HA HA HA HA HA HA!!!
Regards,
Sandra

What do you mean they changed the date? I do not care if it is her birthday! Domenico Pedrazzini takes a back seat to no Queen!
UMM.. Hel-hello?
And what is such a common girl doing in my foyer?
MFFF...
Sir, this is Sandra Arden. Your "discovery" from Rio de Janeiro?
Does not ring a bell! Send her away!
Sir you went to great expense to bring her here. You wanted to "show her freckles to the world."
Mffwhat!?
...
Of course! My freckled beauty! How was your flight?
KISS
TURBULENT!

This deluxe penthouse suite will be your home until you are ready to meet your destiny! Treat it as your own.
It's so big!
Come! You must freshen up after your long flight. The shower is right through here.
Oh, I can wait till later...
Tut tut tut! I insist!
This thing has like a bajillion showerheads!
Oof... I don't know if I'll ever be comfortable with this extravagant lifesty-
Bella? Are you liking the shower?
I want to marry it and have its babies!!!

<Well, what do you think?>
<She is very... plain!>
<And inexperienced.>
<Yes! She is our unspoiled clay, and we will make her a work of art!>
I have never seen Domenico this excited over a model. And certainly not for... *sigh* me!
Oh Domenico, can you not see that I too am a woman?
How I long for the day when you will feel the tender strokes...
...of my whip, caressing your shapely derriere!
Squee! I'm such a romantic!

Whom do you love the most?
Tah-Tatiana!
Louder!
Tatiana!
LOUDER!
TATIANA!
<Wha? Oh! Yes, Domenico?>
<When did you say I must leave for London?>
<Within the hour, Domenico.>
<Very well, I know I can trust you with her training in my absence?>
<Of... of course! You can trust me with anything!>
<Good! This freckled one...>
<...There is something *special* about her...>
KRAK!
What? How dare this gutter-trash bewitch my Domenico's eye? I will destroy her!

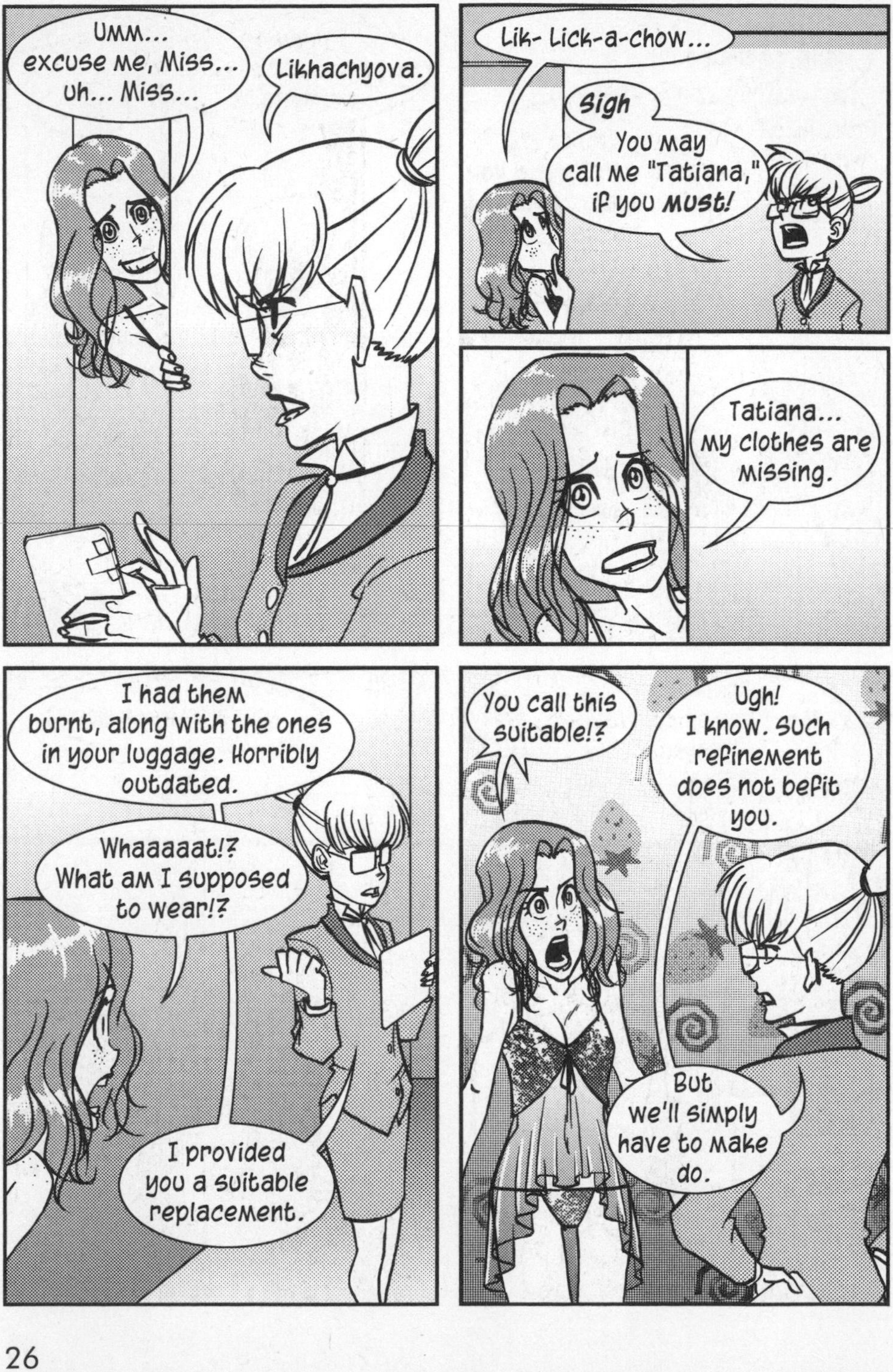
Umm... excuse me, Miss... uh... Miss...
Likhachyova.
Lik- Lick-a-chow...
Sigh
You may call me "Tatiana," if you MUST!
Tatiana... My clothes are missing.
I had them burnt, along with the ones in your luggage. Horribly outdated.
Whaaaaat!? What am I supposed to wear!?
I provided you a suitable replacement.
You call this suitable!?
Ugh! I know. Such refinement does not befit you.
But we'll simply have to make do.

Ah!
Bella, there you are!
Domenico? Where..?
I am on my way to the airport, but I leave you in Tatiana's capable hands.
I promise to take care of her... personally!
Ulp...
Wonderful! I'll leave the introductions to you then.
click
Zoé! Fabien! Meet Domenico's latest "project!"
Ack!
N-nice to meet you.

Fabien is our stylist! He can make anyone look good.
This project will be... a challenge, even for me.
Zoé is a veteran model.
I prefer the term "experienced!" It sounds less... old.
You would do well to listen to her advice.
I... I look forward to learning from you.
Quit now!
What?
Astute as always, I see.

Look at how self-conscious you are! You are not cut out for modeling!
Well I am half-naked in front of strangers, y'know?!
Listen to me! You are nothing! Your body is nothing! Your sole purpose is to make the clothes you wear look good.
If you cannot understand that, then leave now!
I'm not going anywhere!
Domenico returns in a week, if we haven't gotten rid of your body issues by then, you will be of no use to him.
I can do it! I can take anything you throw at me!
Anything?
Y-you're smiling...
Please stop.

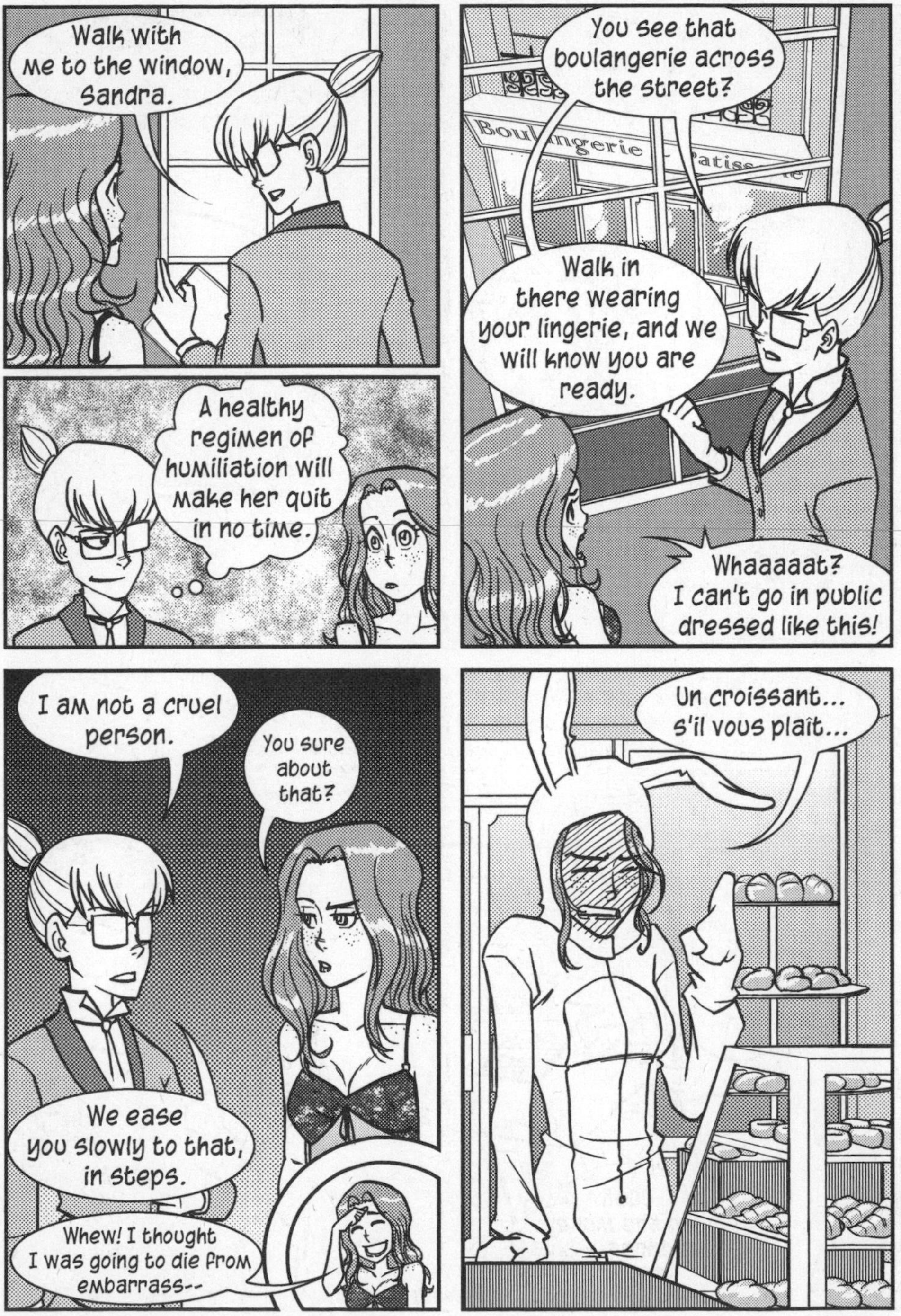
Walk with me to the window, Sandra.
You see that boulangerie across the street?
Boulangerie Patisserie
Walk in there wearing your lingerie, and we will know you are ready.
A healthy regimen of humiliation will make her quit in no time.
Whaaaaat? I can't go in public dressed like this!
I am not a cruel person.
You sure about that?
We ease you slowly to that, in steps.
Whew! I thought I was going to die from embarrass--
Un croissant... s'il vous plaît...

Maman! Un lapin!
Ne regarde pas!
This is sooo humiliating!
But I can do this! I'll show those jerks! Just gotta stay calm no matter what.
Votre croissant, Mademoiselle. Deux euros s.v.p.
Sure.
Just hand the money. Who cares if this guy is...
The most gorgeous slice of mancake I've ever seen!

< Mademoiselle! Please, try a slice of cake. I baked it myself. >
< Oh, I shouldn't... but it does look tasty... >
< It's... divine! I've never sampled such a delicious cake! What flavor is it? >
< Thank you... It is a... >
< Pfft... Carrot cake! >
!!!
Bwaaaaa! I'm so embarrassed!!!
< Mademoiselle! It was a joke! >

I quit!
I quit!
I want to go home!
Excellent!
I'm booking you a flight to Montreal right now.
That was easier than I thought
What?
I can't go on a plane looking like this!
Just wear your other cloth-
oh, right, I burned them...
sniff
Well I can't leave without clothes, can I?
...
Oof!
The chest is so tight!
Who asked you?!

< Mademoiselle! Wait! >
?
< I wish to apologize. I did not mean to offend. You were just so adorable, I could not help but tease. >
< Yeah, well... it doesn't really Matt-->
<You think I'm adorable? >
< Very. In fact, I was hoping I could take you to dinner? >
...
I'm staying!
!?!

Karma Chamelia

You're home late. It's almost dawn.
I had a wonnnnderful time! *hic*
We talked all night! An' he's such a dreamboat!
Whew! I'm beat!
You should get some rest.
I'll wake you when it's time to get to work.
Thaaanks! I thought yew sucked, but yer the *hic* best.
5:45am
Z!
BREE!
BREE!
BREE!
BREE!
!!?
It's time to get to work.
6:30am

But I just got to sleeeep!
I will remind you, you aren't on vacation!
We have a full day's schedule for you. Clean up and get ready for breakfast!
Yeah, yeah...
At least Mr. Ultra Shower will help me relax.
SQUEEK
Bajillion showerheads, do your th--
SHHHHHHHHHHH
By the way, to help you sober up, I shut off the hot water.
YEEEEEEEEEEEEEEEK!!!
Thank me later.

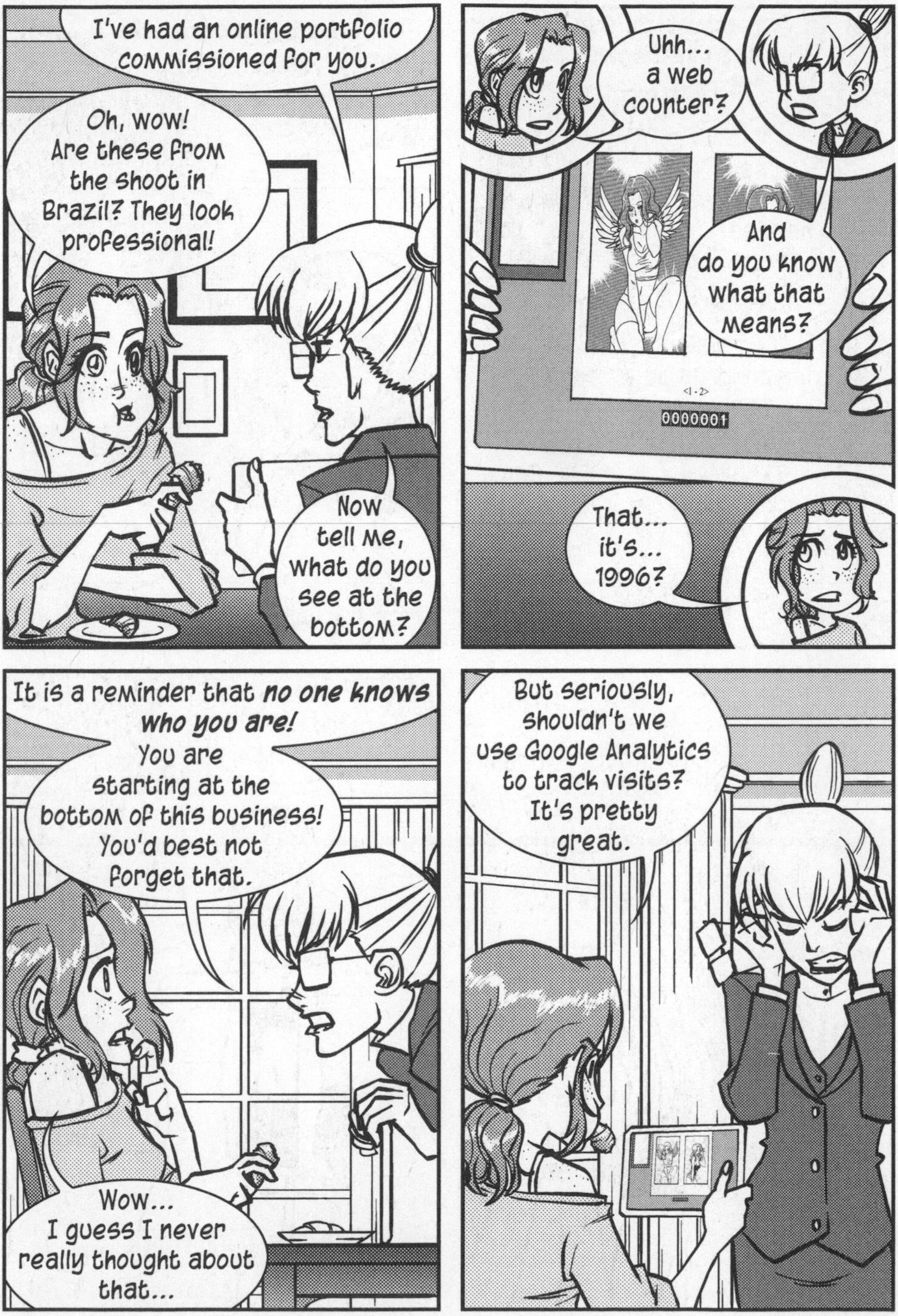
I've had an online portfolio commissioned for you.
Oh, wow! Are these from the shoot in Brazil? They look professional!
Now tell me, what do you see at the bottom?
Uhh... a web counter?
And do you know what that means?
0000001
That... it's... 1996?
It is a reminder that *no one knows who you are!* You are starting at the bottom of this business! You'd best not forget that.
Wow... I guess I never really thought about that...
But seriously, shouldn't we use Google Analytics to track visits? It's pretty great.

Pay attention, Sandra. Your training begins today.
O-okay. Where are we headed?
"Le palais des congrès de Paris."
"Palais"... A... a palace!?
Well, in a manner of--
Oh, nooooo.... I'm not dressed for this!
Your clothing will be provided once there.
Really? How elegant!
This isn't quite what I was expecting.

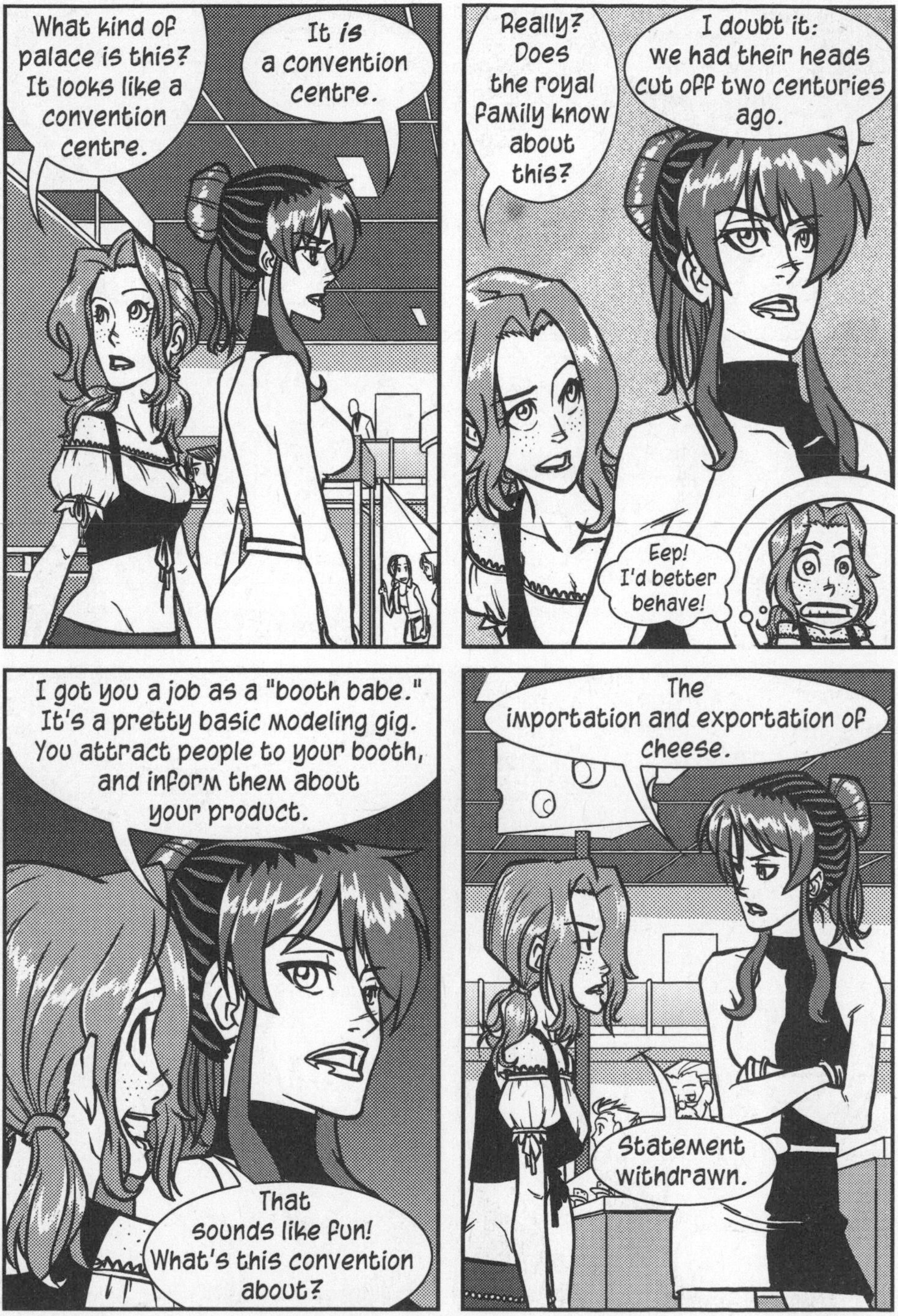
What kind of palace is this? It looks like a convention centre.
It *is* a convention centre.
Really? Does the royal family know about this?
I doubt it: we had their heads cut off two centuries ago.
Eep! I'd better behave!
I got you a job as a "booth babe." It's a pretty basic modeling gig. You attract people to your booth, and inform them about your product.
That sounds like fun! What's this convention about?
The importation and exportation of cheese.
Statement withdrawn.

So what do I even do?
You attract clients with your... ahem adequate figure, and answer their questions about your product.
Sounds boringgg!
Aww... don't be like that... let's see a smile.
...
Aww... You can do better than that. You're so pretty when you smile.
There we go. That wasn't so hard, was it?
Now keep doing that for eight hours!
Eighdt whadt!?

They ask you questions: You smile.
They ask to take a picture with you: You smile.
They pinch your butt (and they will): You smile.
What about punching them? Can I punch them if I still smile?
No!
Here, memorize these facts about your product. And there are free samples back here.
"Imported Polish Gouda & You."
Aw, not Gouda!
Imported Polis
GOUDA
& You
I can't stand the stuff!
The Gouda from the supermarket always tastes so syntheti-
OMG! The supermarkets have lied to me... LIED!

Well, the rest should be simple. I'll check back on you at closing.
Do you have my cell number?
No...
Good.
Zoé, wait! I have another queftion.
Check the manual.
It'f an emergenthy!
I ran out of famples.
GOUDA
<Henri! Change of plans! Give her the stinky cheese!>
Nuuuuuuuuuuuu!

<C-can I take a picture with you?>
<If this is Polish cheese, why are you dressed in German clothes?>
...
FLASH!!
PINCH!

Quitting time! How was your first day as a model?
Awful!
I can't feel my feet, my face or my butt, seeing as it got pinched like a zillion times!
Modeling isn't as easy as you thought, is it?
sniff Promise me I won't have to do this again tomorrow.
Of course you don't.
This event is over! Tomorrow you're a booth babe at the squid trade show.
Whyyyyyyyyyyyyyy?

<As you can see our squids are so fresh they-->
OH GOD IT'S ON MY ARM IT'S ON MY ARM!
<What is the difference between your re-mineralized water and regular tap water?>
H2WHOAH
H2 WHOAH
H2WHOAH
<Ours is in a bottle?>
FLASH!!
DO NOT CROSS
PINCH!
<I dunno... cell phone parts, or something?>
<What does that have to do with body painting?>
<I don't even know anymore!>

<One carrot cake, Pierre, heavy on the frosting!>
Sandra?
<Tatiana watches what I eat like a hawk, so this is between you n' me!>
<Tough week?>
<It was so hard! 12-hour days, on my feet, in high heels! I want to sit down but my butt is numb from the constant pinching! >
<And always with the smiling, no matter how much you want to punch them in their smarmy faces!>
<Smiling! Smiling! Smiling!>
<Well, why don't you stop now?>
<I forgot how!>

<I want you to have this.>
?
<What is this?>
<It's a coupon. Good for one "smile free" dinner. Only frowns or grimaces allowed.>
<Good for tonight only.>
<AAAA! You're the best!>
<Oh! I mean...>
<You're the best.>

<Thank you for dinner, Pierre. I had a wonderfully miserable time.> Tee hee.
<You're welcome, I'm glad you hated it.> Pfft..
Oh! <Before I forget.>
?
SMMOOCH!♡
<Nyaaaaaah! Have a miserable evening!>
<Hope yours is worse! Nyahhh!>

Where are we off to this time?
Video game trade show.
You're kidding! I love video games!
Especially the 16-bit stuff!
Nothing against today's games, but there's something about those simple squares and goofy sounds, you know?
Ooh! Will I get to test the games?
I don't see why not.
Like, all day?
Knock yourself out.

Stupid costume! I can't even play games! And I'm sweating like a pig in here.
<Hey, Mimzy-Molar!>
<Your last three games were stoopid! I want my money back!>
<UMM... I'm just the mascot, kid.>
<Make better games!>
!!!
#$*@&^% kid!
Maman, c'est quoi un "#$*@&^% kid?"
Ne l'écoute pas!

<What do you mean, "You burnt the wig?" It's 15 minutes till showtime!>
<I got nail polish on it, so I tried using lighter fluid to get it out. One thing led to another, then... FOOM!>
<No problem. Just say the character will be blonde.>
<Chamelia is a legacy character! We can't change the hair! You might as well shave Mario's mustache!>
<This is a disaster! The gaming blogs will crucify us.>
<Fft! Chamelia's hair is ugly to begin with. And it's not like there's a suitable replacement nearby.>
Pah! It's so hot in this thing!

<You! What agency represents you?>
<What? I, um... I dunno?>
<We'll worry about the technical details later, get her into costume! She goes onstage in ten minutes.>
What's going on!?
<Whew, thank goodness Mimzy-Molar is one of our parent company's IPs.>
<Hey! What about me? I need to work too!>
<Of course, Eloise. I'll even replace your wig.>

Why do I have double-sided tape on my boobs?
Sorry. The character's costume can't actually stay on without it.
Tell that to my nipples when these get pulled off!
I apologize, but we are desperate.
At least I'm out of that sweaty thing.
What am I now? Some kind of space princess?
You're--
Hey you know, I kind of like this! Reminds me of an old video game with quick-changing outfits.
Carmen Chamelia, yes.
Ch-Chamelia...?
Your moods change quickly too, don't they?
Meanwhile, fourteen years ago:
OUR HEROES
An' that's why Carmen Chamelia is the best video game EVER!
And when I grow up, I'm going to be just like her!

And now from Dark Matter Games, please welcome... Tristan Rambert!
Thank you. As you know, we've been working diligently on the new Carmen Chamelia game.
Our new game focuses on plot and gets to the core of the character, discarding dated, superficial gimmicks...
...like her constant power-switching.
What!?

You can't take Chamelia's powers! That's what makes the game fun! She's like a hundred heroes in one!
...
Ha ha! Yes! that's exactly what the old Chamelia would say. Which is why our new game reveals her gritty past.
Run the trailer.
Did a video game character just argue with its developer?
This presentation is sooooo Meta.

My people captured,
my planet in flames...
My body broken, abused.
Suffering the worst humiliations
at the hands of my captors.
It was then I knew what to do...
SLASH!
STAB!
SPURT!

Guide Chamelia, while avoiding hundreds of realistic deaths, such as impalements!
SHLUNK
Maulings!
SHHRPP
SHHLINK!
And eviscerations!
That's horrible! Girls won't want to play this game!
What? We don't care about girls playing videogames!
Let me go, Alex! I'mmo mess him up!
Marie! No! We'll get banned from the show!

Boooooooooooooo!
Of-of course we care about the female demographic, but in a game of this magnitude, we...
Who here thinks Chamelia should be about changing powers instead of being a snuff film?
Hey!
Yeaaaaaaaah!
Who thinks Chamelia should be a THOUSAND heroes in one?
Yeaaaaaaaaaah!
?
Oh, glob! It's the company's president!

Who here can scream the LOUDEST?
Oh.. H-hello, sir? Oh, y-you're watching the livestream, are you? H-ha... ha...
Give them what they want.
Your segment is going viral. In fact, it's going bubonic.
One cannot buy publicity like this.
Give them what they want, and we will sell millions.
B-but, sir! This game is my opus!
"Your" opus? So it's a game to end your career with, then?
N-n-no, sir.
And who here likes ICE CREAM?

Well... what do you say, "Chamelia..." sh-should we bring back the old you?
Hell yeah, we shoul--
I mean.. if it's not too much trouble...
Then we WILL! But we'll bring you back with high-quality graphics, better sound, and--
FRECKLES!
She looks great with freckles! You put those in and we know you're not just PANDERING!
Yeah! We want freckles! FRECKLES!
RECKLES FRECKLES FRECKLE
Th-the final game will have her looking just like our Chamelia here!
WOOOOOOOO

OMG! You were amazing!
Oh thank y--
Do you have a website?
No...
oh wait...
Yes! SandraArden.com.
But there isn't much th--
You are an inspiration to girl gamers everywhere!
Really? I... Me?
Well, I... I do my part, y'know... I mean, I was just using common SENSE, really... heh-heh... that game was so--
BUMP!
What did you DO?
Eep!

You were supposed to be a mascot, not CAMPAIGN FOR AN EXPENSIVE REDESIGN WHILE DRESSED AS A DIFFERENT--
Yeah buh, um, I...
It's over.
What's over?
This whole "experiment!" If you cannot grasp such a basic concept, I am personally sending you back to--
Um... Excuse me.
Hi, I'm Lavali with Dark Matter Games? I'm here to set up a time for you to come in and model Chamelia for our designers.
Who's your manager?
That would be me.
?

So...
see you next
Tuesday!
Th-
thank
you.
You did make yourself
noticed. Models must do
that. Although your
METHOD was grossly
unprofessional...
Am...
I fired AFTER
that?
...
Sorry,
it just...
happened.
Hm...
perhaps
Domenico was
right...
Perhaps
there is more to
you than meets
the eye.
Really?
No. it
was all
insanely
dumb
luck.
Emphasis
on "dumb."
And possibly
also "insanely."

Geek Chic U

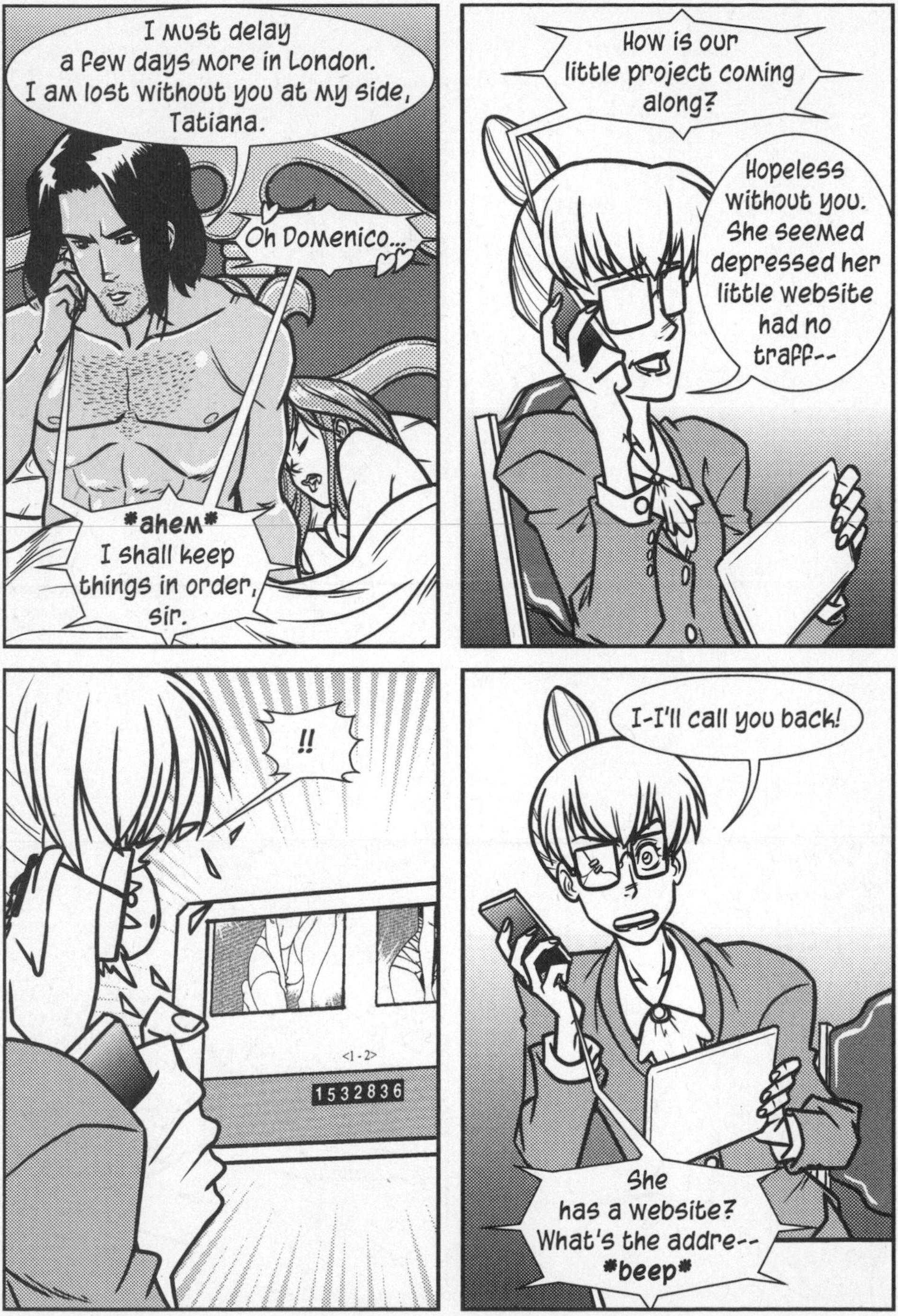
I must delay a few days more in London. I am lost without you at my side, Tatiana.
Oh Domenico...
ahem I shall keep things in order, sir.
How is our little project coming along?
Hopeless without you. She seemed depressed her little website had no traff--
!!
<1 - 2>
1532836
I-I'll call you back!
She has a website? What's the addre-- *beep*

How did you do this!?
Whaaaaaaat? It's too early to get yelled at!
1,532,836 views overnight? Admit it! You inflated the numbers! You... You Google Analyticsed them! Didn't you!?
Here ya go... that should give you the top referrers. *YAWN* Now let me sleep, willya?
...
HOLY CRAP! WAS THAT MY WEBSITE!?

The most referrals come from this video gaming blog.
Huh. How'd they get my address?
They are calling you the savior of girl gamers.
Gosh! I haven't really gamed since high school...
Some coming in from YouTube--
Does... does that make me a fraud? Oh, man! Am I a fraud?
Other gaming sites are picking up the story now.
I gotta go make this right. And I only see one way how.
<One Nintendo, please!>
GUIDE
PSM
EGM

<Nintendo... what? game? System? Plushie?>
<I'M sorry... I'll have a Super Nintendo, please.>
<They... uh... stopped making those in 1999.>
<Oh, okay. What was the name of the new one? The sixty-four something?>
<They stopped making those in 2003.>
<Fine! I'll just have Nintendo's latest system. What's it called?>
<The Wii U.>
...
<No, seriously, what's it called?>

Oh... um... hello?
...
...
I.. um...
I just bought this
Weeyoo, so um... I'm gonna
go play it... if you could
move a bit?
There sure
are some strange
characters in
this shop.
!
!
?

Sandraaaa.... what a pleasure to see you!
Oh my! This is not the Galerie Di Meo...
Uh, no... It's a video game shop.
Oh, you work here now, after failing as a model?
What? Why would you even think--
Do not be saddened! Retail suits you much better.
Have you met my **fabulous** lover, Gary? He's an artist, you know. Very bohemian.
Omigosh! Is that a Wii U?
Bohemians stand quietly, Gary!

It's a good thing you ran into me.
Are you sure price is no object?
Yup! Got a platinum card for business expenses!
Okay! You'll need a couple of Wiimotes and nunchucks in assorted colors for party games.
Oh! Party games! Then some Mario, some Pikmin, Wonderful 101...
You know how to hook this up to your TV?
I... don't even know what kind of TV we have.
Note to self: Find Domenico's TV.
Good news, Senna! We're going over to Sandra's!
How is that good news?!

Well, here we are. Home sweet home.
Whaaaaaat? This is where you live?
Yup, not that I'm here much.
You can't live here! It... It doesn't suit you, It's... It's...
Better than yours?
Better th--
Shut up!
I don't understand! You work in a shop!
I never said I worked there! And things are coming along fine, no thanks to you!
I'm modeling for a video game character now!
Wow! That's so interesting!
Isn't that interesting?
You're so interesting.
Senna! Why did you never say your friend Sandra was so interesting?

Sandra!! You little freckle-faced fool!!
This is what you think passes for professionalism? What were you thinking? What could you possibly have been thinking?
Oh, what am I thinking? You weren't thinking!
...
Why are there strange people in the apartment?

Tuh-tatiana!
Y-you remember Senna!
F-from Brazil!
She brought Gary here to be my... uh... CONSULTANT!
Consultant? What... kind of consultant?
The... uh.. the GOOD kind!
He's here to uh... harness my websites' um... synergy and expand it uhh... exponentially!
Isn't
JAB
that
JAB
right,
JAB
Gary?
Oww... y-yes! Uh... of course!
W-why, if you liked the original Sandra, y-you'll love the new version...
Sandra 2: Sandra Harder!

Well, then... Mister consultant... your client seems to think it is acceptable to usurp her client's presentation.
S-see, she's this video game hero from my childhood, and I just--
S-Sandra...
YOU'RE SO COOL!
THAT is your professional opinion?
WHAT?
I mean... um... Good job, Sandra. Now it's time for me to do my job!
And I'll start by... uh... installing Nintendos!
HNNN...
Your consultant is certainly... unorthodox. Tell me, do you enjoy his services?
Oh, yes. He serviced me so well last night, I may have passed out.
I... see?

Wow, technology has advanced! Look how compact the systems are now.
Actually, that's the controller.
Are you kidding me? This thing is massive!
Okay, hookup is done. Time for the setup.
Let's start by making a Mii.
You're making... a you?
Nono, the Mii will be you, not me.
The you will be me and not you?
No the Mii will be you. That's how Wii works.
How we work?
Well I **can** make a Mii of me, but not the main Mii, which needs to be you, understand?
YOU'RE MAKING FUN OF ME!

You were amazing in that video from the trade show.
I just lost my temper! And suddenly my website's big, and I don't know WHY!
Well, you were pretty "geek chic."
"Geek... sheik?" That means to talk about video games?
Not just games, but movies, comics, animation... you know, geek stuff.
Stuff that you can teach me, right?
?

Come along, Gary time to leave.
Just hold on! Gary's teaching me about geek stuff!
No! It's time for real culture!
Geek culture!
Real culture!
Geek culture!
Real culture!
H-hey... I know... l-let's do both!
Both?
That makes no sense.
T-To Belgium!
?
?

A-CHA KA-CHA KA-CHA KA-CHA KA-
HA KA-CHA KA-CHA KA-CHA KA-C
A-CHA KA-CHA KA-CHA KA-CHA KA-
HA KA-CHA K
To Belgiu-!
HA KA-C
Stop saying that!

Welcome to the Belgian comic strip centre!
Tão absurdo! Why would Gary bring us here?
Unless...
Boo hoo hoo! Gary gave me bad advice that sank my career! I have no choice to become your lowly assistant again!
There, there! At least you know your place.
Gary, you big romantic... are you doing this for me?
During its Golden Age, there were two major schools of art, Hergé's "ligne claire" and Franquin's "style atome."
Poor Sandra. It almost sounds like he knows what he's talking about.

Hey... Senna...
HM?
Is it just me, or are those kids filming us?
Oh! I do believe they are.
Can't be helped, I'm afraid.
My fans follow me wherever I--
Gary! Look! An exhibit on Candy Candy! I used to watch that as a kid!
...

EXCLUSIVE: Sandra Arden seen in Paris buying a Wii U
CPU Overload
http://cpuoverload.com
Savior of girl gamers seen with armful of 1st party title
Spotted in Brussels at Comic Strip Centre
The pictures and footage just keep coming in!
I knew she was the real deal! Blog faster, Alex! Faster!

This is so exciting Alex! We need to tell the world about Sandra!
I know, right?
You find any useable pictures of her on her Facebook?
Just pics of her with family, and in a waitress uniform...
Oh! Here's one with a friend.
Boob job!
Total boob job!
I think they used basketballs for implants.

Oo! Someone sent me more footage from the con!
Hey!
Move over! I want to see it on the big screen!
Be patient, Marie! I'm almost done here!
C'monnnn! This will only take a minute!
So will this!
THUD!
...

Well... this is new.
Huh? What is?
You... Me... Your bedroom floor.
What are you talking about? We used to wrestle all the time as kids.
Y-yeah... but... It's different now!
Yeah, I know. You always won.
That's not what I-- Fine! Finish your stupid article! See if I care!
Gosh! It's a good thing I never won back then.
I had no idea she hated being pinned so much.

Dumb dumb dumb! What was I thinking?
We run a POPULAR blog together! I can't jeopardize all we've accomplished!
So what if I have to turn down other guys who ask me out? I'm past this prince & princess bulljive!
Busy reviewing games here!
You're safe now, my princess.
My hero!
ARRRRRGH! I'M SUCH A GIRL!

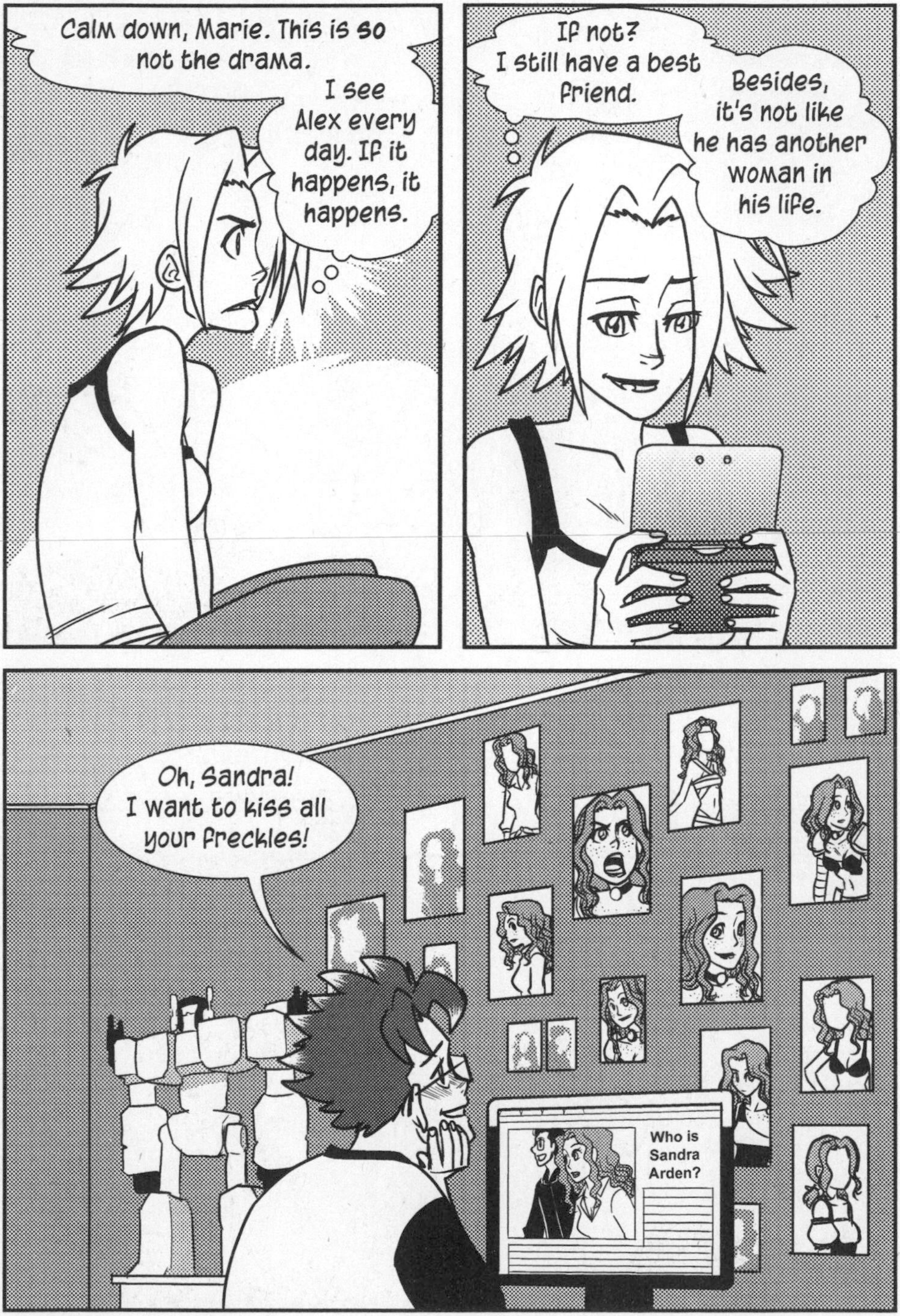
Calm down, Marie. This is so not the drama.
I see Alex every day. If it happens, it happens.
If not? I still have a best friend.
Besides, it's not like he has another woman in his life.
Oh, Sandra! I want to kiss all your freckles!
Who is Sandra Arden?

People were taking pictures of Sandra our entire trip back to Paris, how annoying!
There you are! We're having an impromptu shoot! Change! Now!
?
What the hell is this getup?
Such a gauche outfit! Her humiliation MUST be documented!
Here, take pictures with this.
Gladly.
Oho? Sandra's website... open in admin mode...
HMMMM MMM MMM.

Thanks, Senna. I'm surprised you feel like helpin' out.
Darling, please! I am a professional!
And now to "accidentally" upload these photos to her online portfolio.
OOPS, how UNPROFESSIONAL of me.
And how disastrous for her. No one will take her seriously wearing that.
An X-men cosplay! An X-men cosplay!
I love her more than ever!

Wow, that shoot was... Uh...
Anyway, now let's familiarize you with the Wiimote.
What is this? A sex toy?
Oh, no! It's a controller.
It looks like a vibrator.
It's not a vibrator... though it does vibrate.
So it is a vibrator?
No, it just vibrates to make the experience more intense.
...
It's not a sex toy, believe me.
Okay, okay... I "believe" you.
The first thing we need to do is slide the Wiimote into its latex protection.

It's not working.
You're off to the side. The camera needs to see the sensor bar.
Well, now you're just talking gibberish!
Here... like this.
?
And just swing... and release the trigger...
Gary! It's doing what my arm is doing!
Is it powered by magic?
N-no... just double-A batteries.

Uhhh...
I'll be at the shoot, Esteban. Tchau.
beep
<Enough! I have been patient enough! I wait through the store, the MUSEUM, the photoshoot, the video games, and now I have to leave for work and STILL Gary dawdles!>
What's the matter, Senna? Don't you want to see Gary's portfolio?
You knew he was an artist! Haven't you looked at this?
I'm busy! Very busy! While YOU were playing GAMES, I just got the call for my latest job! I really have to go!
Then go. I can fly Gary back to Montreal.
Y-You'd do that? That'd be great! Isn't she great, Senna?
B-but... we haven't finished our date...
I'm... I'm real sorry, Senna. It... it just didn't work out.
...
...Did I just get dumped?

I'll...
I'll just have your luggage sent here then.
That'd be great! Bye!
SLAM!!
Wow, Gary, I've never seen a man dump Senna, ever. That was pretty badass of you.
Dumped her? I didn't dump her!
...Did I?
Hey Senna, get this, Sandra thinks I d--
Yeah, I may have dumped her.
!

Wow, Gary! You're a really good artist.
Aww, thanks. But I'm not that great...
Hey! I bet if I take you down to Dark Matter Games, I could get you a job. Video games need art, right?
Gosh! You really think so?
Sure! They love me down there.
<Is Tristan all right?>
<He... He keeps making Chamelia jump off cliffs.>

Sorry I'm late, Zoé! Fabien couldn't decide how to style my hair this morning. Not to mention the lineup at the bakery.
!
So? Are we excited to go make video games? Are we excited? I'm excited!
...
Oh, right, sorry! This is Gary.
WHY IS HE IN MY LIMO?

Gary's an artist looking to break into video games, and I just thought--
You. Out.
You're a professional, Sandra! Stop treating this like a school trip!
Well, fine then! You want me to be an "adult?" Then we'll get there ourselves!
I don't need you, or your limo!
SLAM!!
Um.. Can I borrow money for a taxi? I'm kind of broke.
Also, what's Dark Matter Games' address?
...

Domenico, I'm pulling the plug on your little project.
She's not taking her job seriously, does as she pleases, defies authority...
... what's so funny?
Nothing of concern, bellissima, it's just, what you are saying about Sandra...
It reminds me of a certain headstrong model I used to be married to.
...
Just think of her as the daughter you never had.
I hate you.

Zoé? I told you! I'm not getting in your lim--
I need you to drive to this address. There's a substantial tip in it for you If you let me pay up front, no questions asked.
Hey! I said I don't need—
Excuse me a moment.
TAXI!
This cab is going to Dark Matter Games whether you are in it or not. Take advantage of that, or be late and risk losing your job.
...
She... she tricked me!
Are you sure? I think that was her way of being ni--
TRICKED!

<Tristan? Sandra Arden is here.>
Sandraaaa! It's wonderful to see you!
Why hello there, Tristan!
Deep breath Tristan. So we're changing the game & Chamelia's face. It's what the boss wants. At least the changes end there
See, Gary? I told you they love me here.
This is Gary, he's my... uh... personal artist! Models have those, right?
Gary! A pleasure!
Oh! Likewise, I'm sure.
SKETCH
Gary and I have had the best ideas to redesign Chamelia's costume.
TWITCH!!
Ow! That's... quite a grip you've got.

See, it's nothing too drastic. Just a more sensible top.
As an action hero, it's way more practical than having your boobs flop all over when you're fighting.
Yeah, but...
See... this is about dignity, and respect, and the image of women portrayed in games.
SKETCH
I thought it was because you didn't want to pull off painful tape from your nip-OOF!
JAB!

The team's ready for you now, Miss Arden.
Oops! Duty calls! You two can sort out the art details alone, right?
So what are we doing, exactly?
Today, we need to capture your face.
Capture... my face?
Don't worry, it's just us taking a few pictures. It's not scary.
There is nothing about this that isn't scary!

Sitting comfortably, Sandra?
Y-yes.
Good. Now...
GIVE ME YOUR FAAAACE!
!!
Ha ha! Get it? Like Optimus Prime...
f-from the Michael Bay Transformers movies?
That's hilarious!
See? That guy gets it!

I... don't think Chamelia will have those expressions in the game.
But this is fuuuuuuuun!

...so then the game tester says: "Strider? I barely know her!"
Ha ha ha! Stop! You're killing me!
Which makes this part all the harder. We simply aren't hiring any new artists right now.
Oh... I... I understand.
Tough, Gary! That's what friends of Sandra get!
I mean **sure**, your art's great , and **sure**, your style would be perfect for the Amazon-themed game coming out of the NA branch...
And **sure**, my conscience is yelling at me and it sounds like my Mom--
Let me just make a few calls.

I think we have enough for today. Next time we'll do some motion capture. Fun stuff.
Oh, yes... **as a professional model,** I know all about that, haha!
Sandra! Great news! Tristan got me an interview for the art department in the Montreal branch.
Gary! That's wonderful! We should celebrate!
I know, Let's raid Domenico's liquor cabinet.
Are you sure? We could get in trouble...
Aw, what's the worst that can happen?
Sandra's prom night: The worst that could happen.
Honestly, ossifer *hic*, th' bike an' bear waz both inna tree when I got here.
POLI
I think they're's, y'know *hic*... in CAHOOTS.

You got a new job!!
Well, I have an interview... in the Montreal office...
Close enough! We better get Tatiana to book you a flight so you can make it!
Book you a flight? Of course.
It IS the least I can do.
See? I told you there'd be no problem.
That'll be 985 euro.
...

But... couldn't Domenico's company foot the bill?
We are **not** a charity!
If he is Senna's employee, SHE can pay for him.
Still... if he wished to **earn** a ticket... but no, that would be improper.
Sure! I'll do anything.
Anything?
I'm all yours, and ready to work my ass off for that ticket!
Well... there ARE things I've been hoping to test before...
Sh-showing them... to Domenico...
Gary... I don't know about this.
Don't worry, Sandra, I'll just be helping Tatiana with some work.
I'm so happy you feel this way. Now come!
45 minutes later...
So? Ass worked off yet?
YES!

H-hey... I yooshed to think nnnnnintendoland would be a lame game... but for shome reashon it'sh much better than I remember.
Ha! I bet thish ish one game where I can beat the pantsh off of you.
Beat the pantsh off of me? Like... Shtrip Nintendoland?
No, no, like-- *gulk*
Gasp Gary! SHTRIP Nintendoland? I can't believe you'd shink of shumthin' like 'at!
It'j the besht idea I've heared all night!
!!
SMAK!

Whuh?
Ohhh... my hea--
Where're my clothes?
Why am I wearing two layers of clothing?
!!
...
Woo hoo! I won!

Bonjour, Pierre!
<Do you have any burnt croissants? Gary's a little hung over.>
<Sounds like you and your friends had a good time?>

<Well, me and Gary did. He dumped Senna halfway through the visit.>
<Poor Senna. I felt so bad for her.>

<You and Gary, eh? Should I be jealous?>
Tee hee hee!
<Oh, you! You don't need to be jealous of Gary>

D-Do you?

What am I thinking about? Gary's just a friend. A friend!
And it's not like I know much about him!
Prrrrrobably because I spent all our time together making him teach me geek stuff and blabbing about my career.
Nice one, Sandra!
But it's not like I can just forget about Pierre...
HMM... Gary or Pierre...
Gary or P--
Gary AND Pierre!

Bad Sandra! Bad! This is no time to be thinking about Sandra sandwiches!
sigh I should have experimented more in college.
Okay. I need to make a choice here.
I know Pierre a bit. Don't know Gary at all.
So, today will be all about getting to know Gary! See some sights, a nice talk over a candlelit dinner... we'll see where it leads!
We'd better hurry if we want to catch my flight.
Noooooooooooo!

Well... I guess this is it.
Gosh. It's like I have a million things I want to say, but can't think of one.
I... I'm not great with goodbyes.
Yeah... me either...
...
...
Ahh... What the hell!
?
SM
OCH!
Call me!
GUUUUHHHOKAY!

Girls' Night Out

Zzzz....
hnmmm.... puddin' pops...

Flash!
Hnmm... Wha?

Do-DOMENICO!?
Foolish girl! You ruined my shot!

So, uh, boss, why were you taking pictures of me in my sleep? Isn't that kinda unconventional?
And creepy?
Ha ha ha! I like to discover my muses in their most natural states.
Let us forget past indiscretions. My full attention is yours. An entire day of intense photography awaits us.
Wow! That's great... oh... but I have the mocap session today.
Ha ha! Tatiana! Our freckled one speaks in riddles.
"Motion capture." Something to do with video games, I am told.
Puerile nonsense! Dismiss these video game people!
At once, Domenico.
!!
Sandra's motions are mine to capture!
One day, I'll capture yours!
Eh?

!!
Okay... uh... why did I do that? My body just... ACTED!
Mmmmaybe they didn't notice?
Sandra... What is the meaning of this?
Um... I wanted to check my spam folder?
Y-Yuliya...?
Your... spam folder.
It's, um... very good spam. I only get the best!
R-RETURN YULIYA AT ONCE!

Enough tomfoolery, return Tatiana her tablet at once.
Oh! Um... like you mean now, now?
Yuliyaaaaaa....
What's going on here?
Zoé!
Explain yourself!
I.... I'm sorry... I grabbed it without thinking. Domenico told Tatiana to cancel my DM Games gig, and...
Cancel?
Over my dead body!
What!?

She needs this assignment for her personal growth! And you left her training up to me!
Yes! You were training her for MY personal use!
Have you even considered some things are more important than your whims?
No! That would be absurd! My whims are titanic in scope!
Egotistical hack!
Emotionless ice woman!
EMOTIONLESS??
Oh, dear. I have to separate them. This is bad.
Bad how?
QUITE bad.

They've gone past the point of no return! We must run, **NOW!**
PLAP
Holy highballs! Are they fighting or f#%king?
Ahem N-nothing to worry about! This is all perfectly typical behavior!
You mean, this has happened before?
Typically, such blowouts happen once or twice a year.
Wow! Who knew Zoé had it in her?
S-such things are normal. They **WERE** married after all.
Ahhh! Well, that would explain--
WHAT? THEY WERE WHAT?!

Man! they've been at it for an hour now.
CRASH!
Oh, dear. The Ming vase.
How is this going to settle their argument, exactly?
Zoé and Domenico are highly competitive. Each is trying to... "sex" the other into submission. The winner decides the fate of your career.
Can't believe I'm rooting for Zoé to bone Domenico's brains out.
Ha! Domenico is one of the most virile men on earth! Models, starlets, royalty, none can outlast his raw machismo. Face it! Your little "hobby" is as good as--
Grab your coat, we're leaving!
Domenico! No!

Get to the limo before he wakes up.
Couldn't you have gotten dressed, first?
No time!
CLICK CLICK CLICK CLICK
Zoé! Look! A paparazzo!
Wow, I didn't think those still existed. We have camera phones now.
I'll handle it.
...
< I... I'm sorry... It won't happen again.>
< See that it doesn't.>

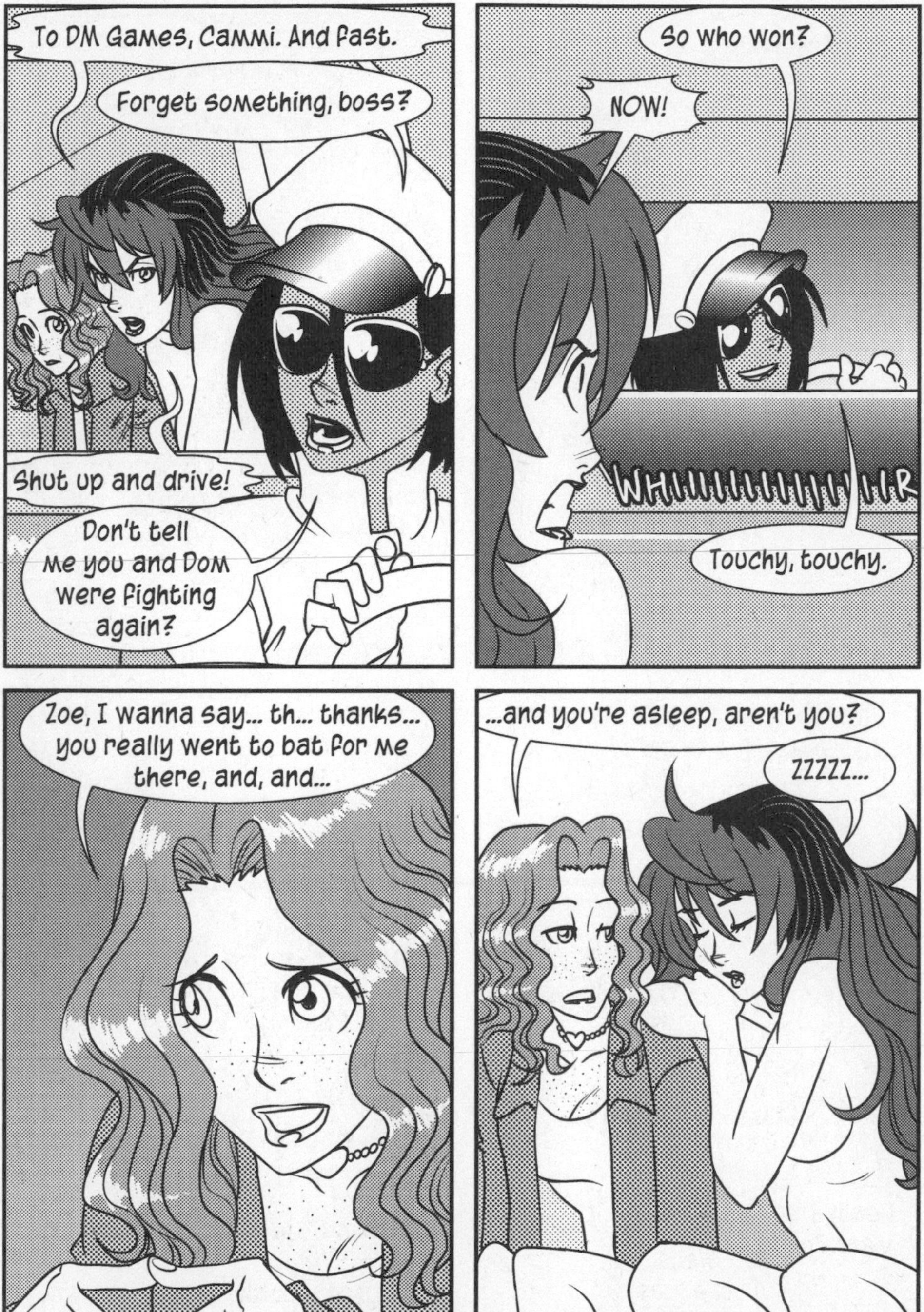
To DM Games, Cammi. And fast.
Forget something, boss?
Shut up and drive!
Don't tell me you and Dom were fighting again?
So who won?
NOW!
WHIIIIIIIIIIIIIIR
Touchy, touchy.
Zoe, I wanna say... th... thanks... you really went to bat for me there, and, and...
...and you're asleep, aren't you?
ZZZZZ...

Hey! Freckles!
Ahh! Limo ghost!
Now that the boss is passed out, how 'bout you lower the privacy window so we can get to know each other better?
How did you know Zoé fell asleep?
Security camera. Lets me know if there's trouble, or someone's head needs bustin'.
You mean we're being recorded?
Naw! No tape. Too bad, tho'. This limo's seen its share of action.
Really! You mean Zoé?
Well... she was THERE...
...
Five more minutes, boss...
Or better make it ten... you know how he is.

Wow! You and Domenico?
Puh-lease, Freckles! Me and Dom, it's a casual thing.
Wait... are you why they split up?
Naw! That was years after they parted ways.
That doesn't explain why she didn't fire you.
Eh... good chauffeurs are hard to come by... and baby, I'm just. That. Damn. Good!
I'm, um... I'm Sandra, by the way...
Cammi.
Sorry I never spoke to you before, I wasn't sure if I had to tip you or not.
Oh, you do. In fact you owe me close to a grand by now.
Whaaaaaaaat!?
Gawd, Freckles, you are so gullible!
You b... Meanie!

By the way, not that it's not a good look on you, but are you really going into work in your jammies?
My... ACK!
Oh nooooo..... Zoé was so naked, I forgot I needed to change! What'll I doooo?
Re-lax, Freckles! Zoé keeps a spare set of clothes in the limo. It's in the cupboard behind you.
You're a lifesaver, Cammi!
Um... hi, I'm here for the mocap session.
Oh! Sandra! We were just getting ready for y--
You know.... most people wear sweats to these things.
...I guess they just don't have a sense of style?

You can get changed in here.
Thanks. Say, would you mind bringing a Gatorade or something to the limo?
I think Zoé needs to replenish her electrolytes.
I'm on it.

H-hello? is someone there?
I'm warning you... I've got a... a....
Designer dress.
Huh... Guess I was imagining things.
Omigosh! omigosh! I can't believe I get to work with you! I'm soooo excited! Are you excited?
!!
Of course not, you must do this all the time! I mean... d'uh! Right? Oh wow, your eyes are green!

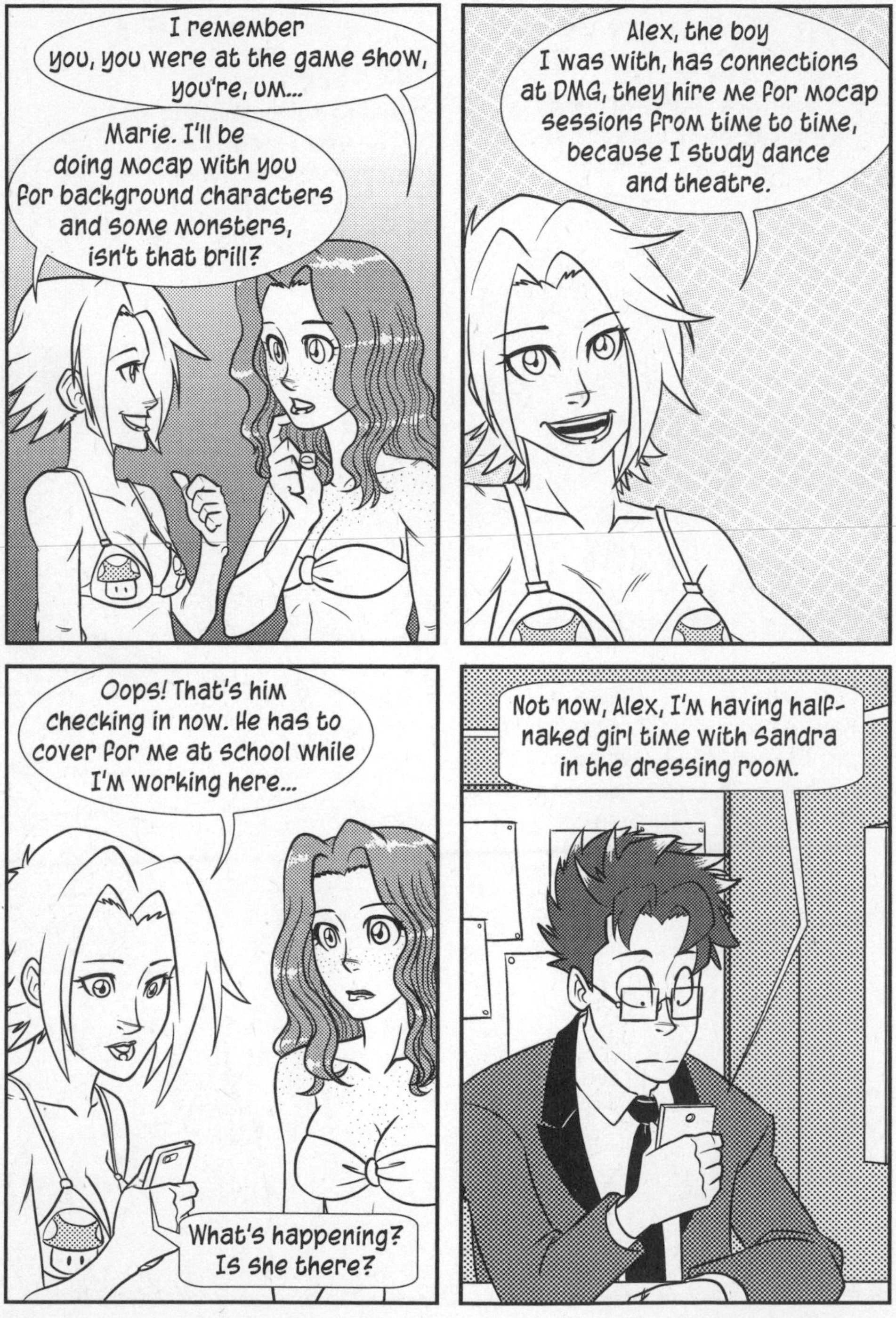
I remember you, you were at the game show, you're, um...
Marie. I'll be doing mocap with you for background characters and some monsters, isn't that brill?
Alex, the boy I was with, has connections at DMG, they hire me for mocap sessions from time to time, because I study dance and theatre.
Oops! That's him checking in now. He has to cover for me at school while I'm working here...
What's happening? Is she there?
Not now, Alex, I'm having half-naked girl time with Sandra in the dressing room.

Wow, you're, uh... bendy.
I've been so nervous that I've been doing stretching exercises since this morning.
Y-you have?
Sure! Don't want to pull something on the set, I mean... how embarrassing would **that** be?
Ulp!
Not that I have to tell a pro like **you** that.
Ha ha HA! Of course not! But to be on the safe side, why don't you show me your routines?
UNCLE! UNCLE!
Haha! You're such a kidder, Sandra.

<Hello? Sandra asked me to bring you a sports drink.>
<This is the right limo, isn't i->
<Iiiiiiiiiiiiiiiiiiiiiiit?>
<Your clothes! Give them to me!>
!!?
EEEEEEEEEEK
What did I say? Never a dull moment in here.
"I was listening to my iPod, officer, I didn't hear a thing..."

Annnd... now we're in space outfits. Appropriate, I guess...
Ooo... Here comes that girl-gamer-hating Tristan. I ought to thump him proper!
You could.... or you could keep your job.
Don't worry, I'm **loads** mature. I know how to act professional.
Good morning, girls, thanks for coming in today.
Our pleasure... Tristan!

Ah! Ladies, are you ready to mocap?
Raring to go, Julien!
We'll also be filming on a camcorder for behind-the-scenes stuff we can put online.
I want to review that footage before it's made public.
Zoé!
O-of course, you needn't worry. Lavali is a pro at this.
Say... Where is Lavali?

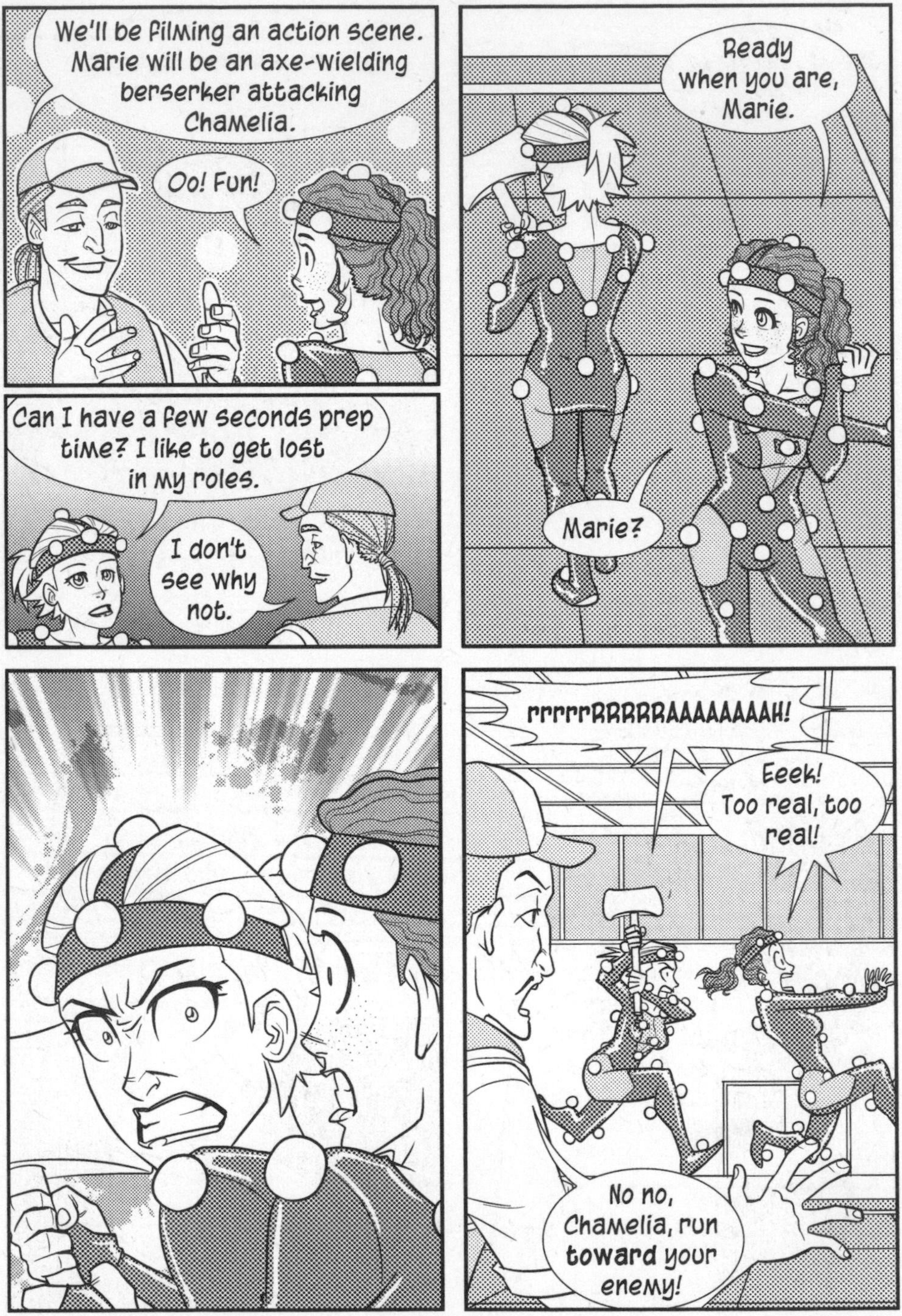
We'll be filming an action scene. Marie will be an axe-wielding berserker attacking Chamelia.
Oo! Fun!
Ready when you are, Marie.
Can I have a few seconds prep time? I like to get lost in my roles.
I don't see why not.
Marie?
rrrrrRRRRRAAAAAAAAH!
Eeek! Too real, too real!
No no, Chamelia, run **toward** your enemy!

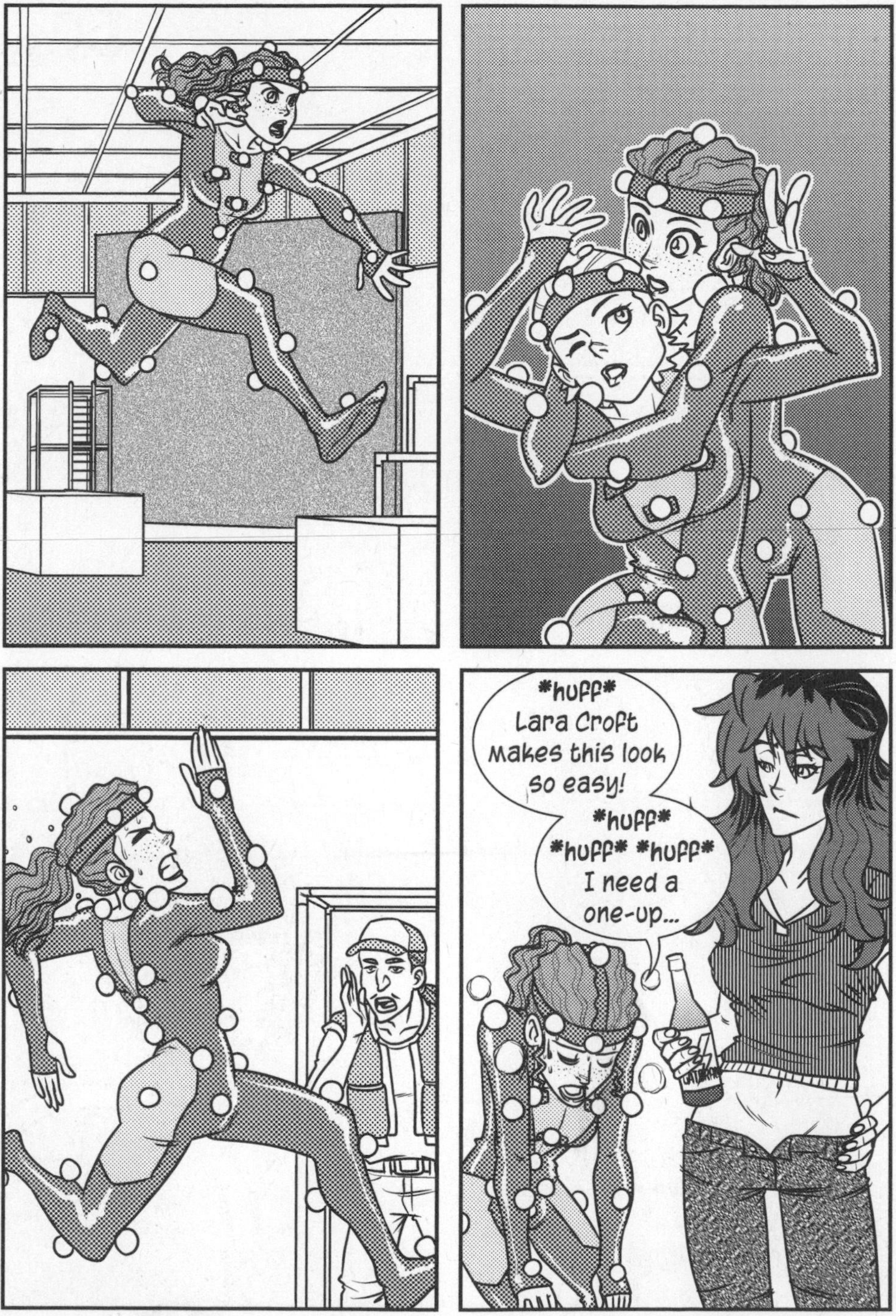
huff
Lara Croft
Makes this look
so easy!
huff
huff *huff*
I need a
one-up...

TMP
?
Clothes? but... where did...?
Never liked that uniform anyways.

Oof!
Hope I did okay out there.
Are you kidding? You were smashing!
I'M surprised to see you in here Zoé, I'd have thought public showers were beneath you.
They are!
Do you want me to wash your back? N-not that i think your back is gross or anything.
I just need to get the stench of ex-husband off of me.
Domenico! I forgot all about him! Do you think he'll be angry?
We'll re-negotiate the terms of your activities, once he recovers.
R-recovers? From what!
D-don't worry, Domenico! Y-you'll get her next time! For the good of the company, I offer you my body for practice.
Bellissimaaaaaa....

You were great out there, Sandra!
Yeah... but you were better.
Don't say that, I was rubbish, really...
No, you weren't.
I know potential when I see it.
Th-that's very kind, but I'm just a student...
Have you ever thought about modeling?
M-me? A model?
If you want to pursue it, I suggest you give me a call.
Y-yes! Absolutely.. I- I will consider doing that, maybe, possibly!
I'd give you my card, but as you can see, I'm naked.
What? You're naked? Y-you can barely tell!
Sandra! Did you know she was naked?

I'll be taking my dress back.
Oh... Okay... But what'll I wear?
You didn't bring clothes, Sandra?
There was a bit of a "wardrobe mix-up."
Oh... Well, why don't we find some DMG promotional clothing?
That's genius, Marie!
Squee!
Zoé, let's go ask Lavali!
That might be a problem.
YOU DID WHAT!?
!!

Ahem...
Lavali? What are you wearing?
I brought you this shirt seeing as you saw fit to strip me naked.
Zoé!?
If you needed clothing, we could have arranged--
Zoé, what the hell did you--
I'm confused... What happenned?
Normally I should press charges...
I'm so sorry, this is MY fault...
But to maintain good relations between our companies...
Can we start over? I could use this on my blog...
ALL OF YOU! IN MY LIMO!
NOW!

MARCH! MARCH! MARCH! MARCH!
Hey, boss, bet you're wondering why I'm naked in your limo again--
No!
Fair enough.

Sh-she's YOUR boss! What's she going to do to us?
I don't know! I've never seen her like this!
I shouldn't even be here, I should jump out of the car, why can't I move--
GRAB
Poor kid. She must be scared out of her mind.
AAAAAAA! I can't believe we're riding in a limousine!
A proper one!
Selfie!

Aaaaaa! Pinch me! I'm dreaming!
This is one of Paris' trendiest boutiques! I never dreamed of walking in here for fear of going in debt for life!
Simone.
<Zoé. Interesting company you keep nowadays.>
<Yes... It seems I owe a debt to one of them.>
<I need you to make them presentable, as I plan to take them out clubbing tonight.>
<On my tab, naturally. I trust this is acceptable?>
<Yes! You're forgiven! You're so forgiven it's crazy!>
See? The boss is just a big softie at heart.
What part of "wait in the car" was unclear to you?

<I got your emergency text, Zoé. May I presume you've arranged an impromptu shoot for our little "experiment?">
<No shoot today, Fabien.>
<Then why, pray, are you wasting my valuable time?>
<I need you to make some girls look good to go clubbing.>
<Darling! Please see my previous question! I am a professional! Not some gossipy hairstylist from a cheap salon!>
<You will do this because I asked! These girls will be seen with me, and I do not do things halfway!>
<You? Clubbing with friends? Have I walked through a time warp when I entered the shop?>
<Very well. The novelty alone is worth my fee.>
<It's true. I rarely go clubbing these days. I have other recreations.>
<Crushing insolent stylists, for example.>
<I meant you having friends.>

Whoof, my hair's a mess.
WHISK
WHISK
Sandra! Darling!
Sandra! Darling! Let me take care of th--
EEEEEEEK!!
Hm, wrong stall.
N-next stall...
WHISK
Sandra!
WHISK
San--
Oh... It's you!
Hey, sailor. Enjoying the show?
EEEEEEEEEEEK!!
Oh, this is the first stall again.
Dammit, Simone, your shop's a maze!

Sandra! Darling!
Fabien! Darling!
Did you wash your hair without conditioner? I warned you about that!
Sorry... I didn't think I'd need to shower on the job.
Incorrigible! I'll have to work miracles as usual. I'll fetch my tools.
S-Sandraaaaa.... He saw Peach and Daisy...
Aww... Sorry, Marie. Um, if it makes you feel better...
I'm mostly certain he might be gay.

Nice! So? Where are we headed?
You're not coming!
It's cute that you believe that.

Aaaa... look at me! This is amazing, I look so posh!
I told you, Fabien is a miracle worker.
You're the best!
Ladies, please! I do not react well to praise, even if it is 100% true.
I trust this is all to your satisfaction?
So much yes!
Then I trust I will not see anything about my indiscretions on your video game blog?
Blog? What blog? I don't even like video games!
That was a fib! Don't believe it! I think video games are totally fab!
Uh, I know, Marie. You make it pretty obvious.
PHEW!

Lavali! Lavali! Take a picture of me and Sandra! I want to send it to your brother.
Sure.
?
VTT
VTT
Hey, Alex! Check these babes out!
Wow! Sandra looks amaaaaaaazing!
Who's that other girl?
P.Yo!!
P.Yo!!

Here we are.
Cor blimey! Th-this is Eviv Bulgroz!
Y-you didn't say we were coming to one of Paris' top nightspots!
?
The proprietor is a friend of mine.
This is so ace, I could die!
Th-this is too fancy for someone like me... I should go wait for you all behind a plant or something.
Let's get you some drinks, to calm you down.
Sandra! Try not to embarrass the company!
Puh-lease! I can hold my liquor like a champ!
Don't you just hate lippy employees?
Didn't I tell you to stay with the car?
No problemo! One limo on the dance floor coming up!
Sigh You can stay... and yes... they are the worst!

You're the chauffeur, right?
Zoé might argue that point, but last I checked.
So... um... that chauffeur's uniform, i-in the car... that was yours?
Naw, it was probably the limo fairy.
Th-thanks for that... it was mighty decent of you.
Hey, don't worry about it. I've been meaning to take up nudism anyways.
Y-you didn't peek, did you?
Re-laaaaax, legs, you're not my type.
I'm into redheads.

Zoé.
Éva.
I'm surprised to see you here. You must be pushing 33, you're practically a fossil by now.
Is that your protegé? So... innocent-looking. It'd be a shame if one of your rivals were to strike at you through her and squash her career before it started.
Quite...
Just as it would be a shame if pictures of you with your original nose "happened" to surface.
I don't actually have any pictures, but you'd be surprised how often that line works.

It's just Gary knew all these cool geek things, right? An' me, I don' know nothin', nothin'.
I should give you my brother's email. He's an expert on that.
Oh, cool, thanks. You're cooool. Send me yours too! We should hang out... 'n' stuff.
Aw, I'm not that cool, really, but sure, I'll--
Hey, c'mon, Freckles. Let's show these tightasses what it means to sexydance.
Sexydance? I'm not drunk enough to sexydance!
'Kay, now I am!

That's the way, Freckles, we're gonna set this place on fire with pure sexy.
Niiiiice improv.
Okay... big finish.
Take my top off and cover my boo-- Freckles?
What... WHAT?
Yo, Freckles? Over here.

Sexy daaaaaance!
You! This is your doing!
Sandra, put those down this instant. Heaven knows where they've been.
SLAP!
!
What sickens me is that you sent your underling to do your dirty work. You didn't even have the guts to attack me yourself.
...
As you wish.
Let go of meeeee...
Sexy daaaaaance!

SPLASH!!
Let that be a lesson.
Auuuuuuuugh! I hate you!
Sexy daaaaaaaaaaance
...
SPLASH!!

<Wooooo! Ev'rbody skinny dip!>
<Now this is a party!>
SPLASH!!
...
<Cannonball!>
SPLASH!!
<Out of my way!>
SPLASH!!
sigh
<Me first!>
SPLASH!!

Sh-should we do it?
D-do you want to do it?
Everyone else is doing it.
It would seem weird if we didn't do it.
SPLASH!!
We did it!
We're doing it!
WE'RE NAKED IN PUBLIC!!!
Ahhhhhh! We're naked in public!

Admit it, boss: you're having fun.
Don't be absurd. I couldn't be seen being left out. I have a reputation to maintain.
Sure, sure.
<C'mon baby, let's have a look.>
<Dude! Personal space!>
<C'mon, don't be shy.>
Nooooooooo!
POW!
...
See, I told you you were having fun!

Tsk tsk tsk.
Getting kicked out of Eviv Bulgroz for rowdy behavior.
Not another word.
I can't take you anywhere.
Tonight was a little too wild for me... but it was nice to go out for a change.
When Sandra's around, everthing is wild... and glamorous!
WOOOO
We should hang out more. Le'ss hang.
I bet you were the most popular girl in high school.
Nahhh! I was plain. No one noticed me, really.
As if!
"I can't imagine anyone out there not liking you."
Sandra Arden.
I will destroy you.

Bonus Story

TWISTED TUESDAY
Written by David Lumsdon
Drawn by Eisu
Up! You have work to do.
I don't wannaaaaaaaaaa!

Stop being a child. This isn't a holiday resort.
I want a break! I was on my feet all day for the past five days! Grinning like a moron all the while!
Please! Like your job is so hard. You don't even know what real work is!
Hey! I used to be Senna's assistant, remember? Compared to that, I could do your job standing on my head!
YOU wouldn't last five minutes in MY job! You'd be all: "Oo! Where are my schedules? What is this 'smiling' thing you speak of?"
My MBA more than overqualifies me for--
Ha! Most interesting!
Do-Domenico?
Your walking a mile in each other's shoes would prove amusing.
Please tell me you're not actually suggesting--
I approve this!
sigh

Sandra Arden, reporting for duty, Domenico.
Ha ha ha! Very good.
So what's first on the agenda?
Kindly inform my "guest" from last night that I shan't be spending the day with her.
!!
Just inform people of the product.
I have already successfully committed the information docket to memory.
Good, because I'll be keeping these!
And do try to keep composed when you get pinched.
What do you MEEEEP!
PINCH

Af-after everything he whispered last night, now he wants me gone?! Men are such pigs!
Yeah, like my ex who cheated on me... with another man! I say you DON'T leave and really make him suffer!
Would this product look good on my figure?
Would it clash with the pattern on my blouse?
Hey, can you even SEE us over here, or do you need glasses?
PINCH
Of course Domenico would be happy to host--
No, wait... he has a gallery opening that d--
And three shoots scheduled at the same time?
TABLETS! WHY ARE THERE NEVER ENOUGH TABLETS
The models
WHAP
Are not!
WHAP
For touching!
WHAP

Th-that wasn't so hard.
N-not at all...
I bet I could keep doing your job for weeks.
I... c-could do yours for months.
Who am I kidding? I hate your job!
I hate your job!
I hate yours more!
I never want to do yours again!
L-look... maybe you've earned just a little--
Oh, let's just drop this and forget it forever.
Sandra can, but it seems Tatiana has gotten some repeat business.
?
Have you been a naughty businessman this week?
F-forgive me, mistress!
End

Baking with Fury

So, after negotiations--
Vigorous negotiations.
It was decided that I shall be in charge of your career, but you shall work on Domenico's projects when available.
Kay.
In the mean time I've lined up more work for you at trade shows.
Moaaaaan!
I suppose it's a small price to pay to keep living in this luxurious apartment.
Also, you'll be moving out, effective immediately.

Muh-move out? But I love it here!
Precisely. A model needs HUNGER to succeed. From now on you'll be paying your own way with the money you've earned.
As per your request I found a hovel-- *ahem* "apartment" that is particularly... "rustic."
Yes, very good.
Do not worry, my freckled beauty! You will not be lonely.
I won't?
Of course not! Tatiana will be moving in with you!
WHAT!?

M-me? Move in with... HER... into THAT?
I need someone I trust to look after my investment.
A direct order from Domenico. I MUST obey. And yet...
Sh-she has failed you, sir! She has proven unwilling to work hard enough to be a model!
Hey! I'm already a champ model!
Need I remind you, you never passed my simple test of buying croissants in your underwear!
Ha! Is THAT all? I'll go buy some right now, COMPLETELY NAKED!
U-under these bedsheets...

Ack!
Oh, good, I can use my reflection in these tinted windows to fix my sheets.
Good thing no one's here to see this.

<No bunny costume today?>
<I... I'M here to prove my worth as a model.>
<I thought you were here for a toga party.>
<Ha ha, very funny, "Monsieur.">
<I don't understand why they keep making you "model" things no one would actually wear.>
<Just give me the usual. And throw in a nice tartelette, so I can rub it in Tatiana's smug f-->
SNAG
meep

Noooooooooo!
<L-Let me get you some clothes.>
IDIOT! Why did I have to one-up Tatiana? Pierre just saw me-- Ahhhh! I could just die!
Don't look at me, I told you to wear lingerie.
I'm n-not like Zoé... she was so confident, she could walk around naked in the street.
But... M-maybe I sh- should try to PRETEND I'm--
Regarde Maman! La fée des pains!
<Look Mommy! The bread fairy!>
Ne regarde pas!
<Don't look!>
NOPE!

<H-here you are... it may be a little big but... S-sorry this happened to you.>
<Thanks... but don't be. It's all for my career, you know?>
<Not really, but okay.>
<You're such a gentleman, Pierre. I know some guys who would've used this chance to make fun of me or, you know... make a move?>
<You are safe with me, Sandra.>
<Thanks. But you know... I suppose making a LITTLE move would've been all right...>
...
CRASH!
OUR
PLOOMF

<Well... That was new.>
<That was wonnnnnderful.>
<Perhaps it is something we should do more often?>
giggle <Mmmmmaybe?>
<Mmm... This is so nice. I've forgotten why I came here.>
<To buy a croissant... and a tartelette, non?>
<Oh, yes. I'll have those,> s'il vous plait?
<That will be three euro, please.>
...
?
I forgot to bring money.

Yes! Yes! This look is perfection!
These will be tasteful, right?
I have found my freckled muse!
Grr... I suppose this means she passed my test.
Yes, and it appears our little protégé has also stumbled into her first magazine cover.
WHAT!?
THWAK!
La sauveuse des gameuses.
Hmm...qu'est-ce--?
<MY TABLET!>

Ten days earlier...
Grr... lousy, heavy, sweaty costume! I was supposed to be up on stage! Who does that girl think she--
There you are.
Omigosh! It's-- it's Zoé Duchateau!
I came to check up on you.
M-Mz Duchateau... I-it's a great hon-
Who thinks Chamelia should be about changing powers--
WHAT? What's that little fool doing onstage? That wasn't her assignment!
Oof!
She stole my gig AND my idol! Ooooooooo!

<Tsk, you've damaged the screen. Now I'll have to get Daddy to buy me a new one.>
<Ooooo! I hate her! I hate her! I haaaaaaate her!>
<Who?>
<That red-headed excuse for a model!>
<She stole my gig from the trade show, and they put her on a cover for it? That should be **me** on that cover, Nadine!>
<So angry! So **PASSIONATE!**>
HMMM...
< I bet I know how to make you forget all about that nasty redhead.>
<She has to have a website or something? Facebook? Twitter? Arrrrgh! Who is she?>

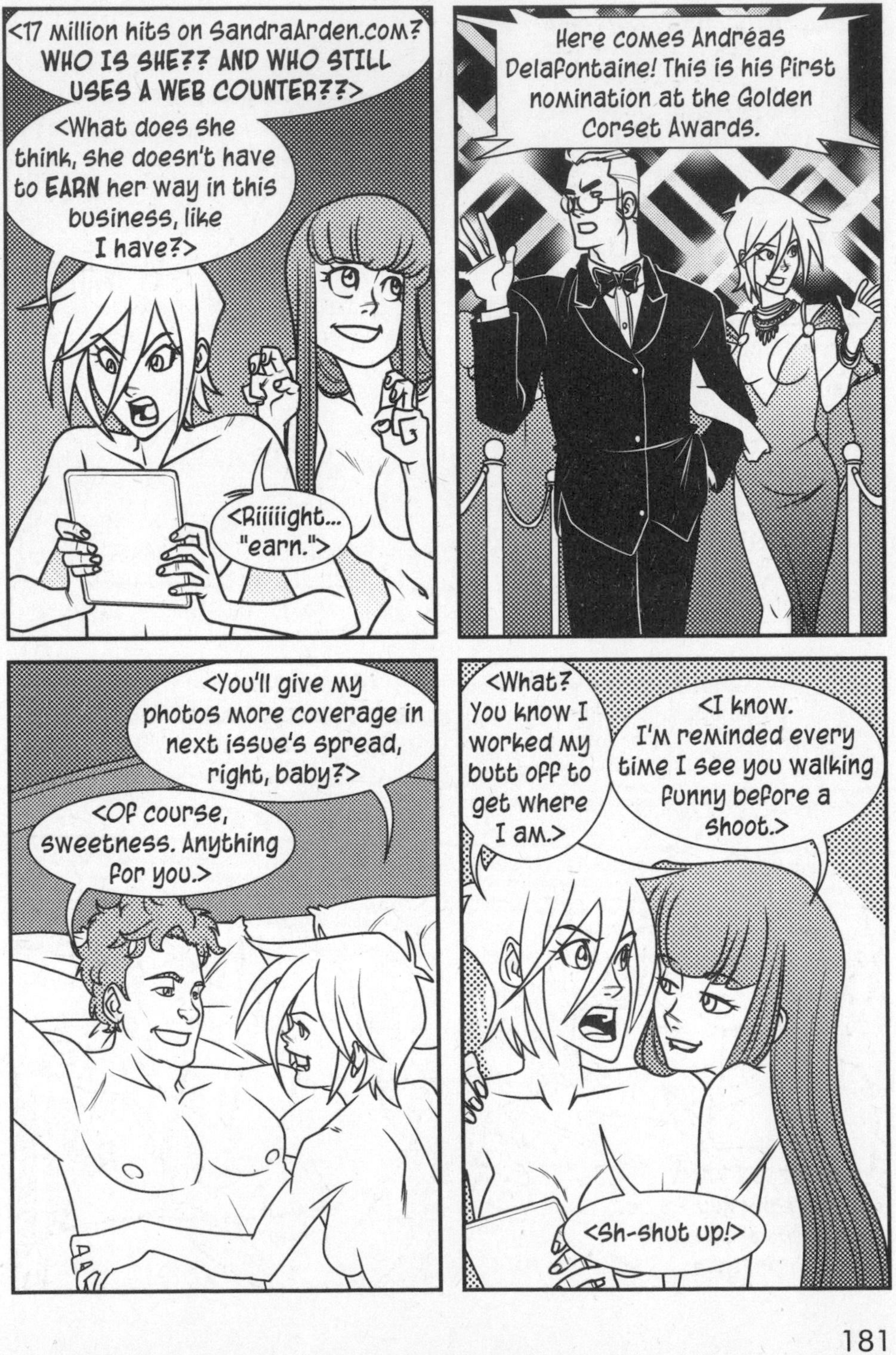
<17 million hits on SandraArden.com? WHO IS SHE?? AND WHO STILL USES A WEB COUNTER??>
<What does she think, she doesn't have to EARN her way in this business, like I have?>
<Riiiiight... "earn.">
Here comes Andréas Delafontaine! This is his first nomination at the Golden Corset Awards.
<You'll give my photos more coverage in next issue's spread, right, baby?>
<Of course, sweetness. Anything for you.>
<What? You know I worked my butt off to get where I am.>
<I know. I'm reminded every time I see you walking funny before a shoot.>
<Sh-shut up!>

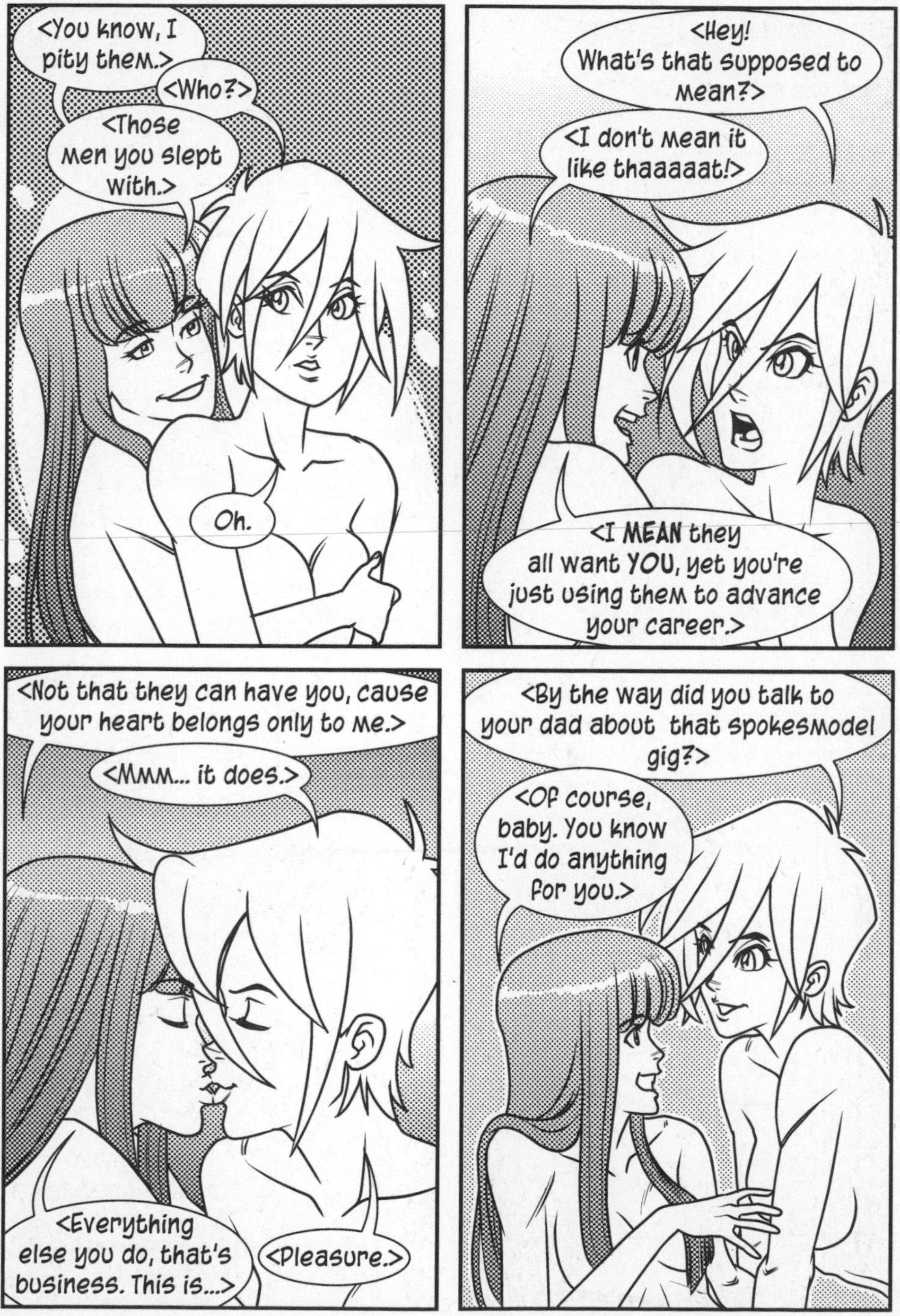
<You know, I pity them.>
<Who?>
<Those men you slept with.>
Oh.
<Hey! What's that supposed to mean?>
<I don't mean it like thaaaaat!>
<I MEAN they all want YOU, yet you're just using them to advance your career.>
<Not that they can have you, cause your heart belongs only to me.>
<Mmm... it does.>
<Everything else you do, that's business. This is...>
<Pleasure.>
<By the way did you talk to your dad about that spokesmodel gig?>
<Of course, baby. You know I'd do anything for you.>

<You know, you're lucky I'M not the possessive type.>
Mhm.
<Sometimes I think you take me for granted.>
Mhm.
<Want to go clubbing tonight?>
<Can't, baby, I've got a night shoot. Some other time?>
<Humph! You **are** taking me for granted.>
<Just for that, I'M gonna go seduce that boy you like!>
<Wh-- Nadine, no! Nadine get back here!>

<Nadine, don't you dare-->
<Think he'll like my new dress? Daddy flew it in for me from Milan.>
<Not that I expect it will stay on me for very long.>
<I swear to Vogue, Nadine!>
<Can you picture it, Eloise? His sweaty naked body writhing next to mine,>
Grr...
<all>
<night>
<long?>
<We should probably take pictures!>
<You know some photographers, right?>
Eek!

<What? It's not like you ever made a move on him.>
<I just... never found the right moment.>
<Your entire lives is "not the right moment?">
<It's not that simple. He's always been there for me, since I was little. It's like... a perfect love, y'know? Like in a fairy tale.>
<Just remember whose poison apples you eat at night.>
<Besides, how do you tell your cousin you're in love with him?>
<Hunph! I'm getting a little jealous over this "love" you have for him.>
<But forbidden love is so **HOT!**>
<Well, it would be forbidden if this were Paris, **TEXAS!**>
<FORBIDDEN LOVE IS HOT!!!>

<Nadine, why are you doing this?>
< Who's to say? Are you still angry about that redhead?>
<Huh... I guess I'm not...>
<Mission accomplished.>
ulangerie - Patisseri
<C'mon, I'm starving! Let's get some of your Cousin Pierre's famous croissants.>

B-bonjour, Pierre...
<Huh, that's odd... is that a bedsheet on the floor?>
<And look, uniforms on the floor.>
<Hey... do things look like they've been knocked over?>
<Do you think there's been a break-in?>
CLATTER
Pierre?
Oh Sandra! Oh Sandraaaaaaah!

<Sandra? That's not "the" San-->
<Oh baby, I'm so sorry!>
...
<Baby? You okay? You haven't said a word the entire ride home.>
...
<I'm going to need your printer... a-and some candles...>
<Sure, baby, whatever you want...>
<Uh... what for?>
Sandra Arden, I will destroy you.
<Annnd back to square one.>

Pumped

So Alex, are you ready for my final smash... of love?
Romance has joined the battle!
Mmmm... Sandraaaaa... romance has... zzz
Tmp tmp tmp tmp tmp
Up!
!!

Owww! What the heck, sis?
You're not sleeping till noon again, Alex. I need your help around here.
Cut me some slack, Lavali. I was up all night podcasting with game devs for our blog.
I can't help it if they are all in *yawn* inconvenient time zones.
I'M serious, Alex. I need you for--
Tmp tmp tmp
No, I'M serious. I'M going back to slee--
Out of bed, lazybutt.
!!

Put your kit on, Alex! From now on, we're jogging every morning.
What? Why?
It's the first step to getting in shape, so we can get nice and strong.
That idea sounds bad... "Atari Jaguar" bad!
Aw c'mon Alex, don't you want a six-pack?
Marie! I'm a gamer! How would having abs help ME?
You never know-
Bam! Another victory! You know the rules, Alex...
Lose the shirt!

Alex, about that task I need you f--
Find someone else to do it.
This is serious, Alex. One of our clients, Sandra Arden, needs a consultant in gaming culture.
WC
!?
Oh! I might be seeing more of her through work stuff. I may as well do it, I suppose.
WC
That'd be great. Let me give you her phone number.
!!
Mine!
!?
WC
!?

Alex... what was that about?
I... uh.. I mean...
Marie, what with your schoolwork, dance lessons AND your game reviews, I'd be afraid of you burning out. Please, allow me to lighten your burden.
Well... if you insist...
Yes! Haha, VICTORY! If my heart were going any faster right now, it would EXPLODE!
And now that you're up, let's exercise!
Noooooo!

You want us to jog up and down stairs?
Sure! Twice the effort, twice the results. We'll be strong in no time.
5 minutes later
Huff Huff
You're not slowing down, are you? We've barely broken a sweat!
10 minutes later
Huff T-try and k-keep up... W-with--
Wheeeeeze!
You want to *Huff* go play *Huff* video games?
Dear God, yes!

hah *hah*
hah *hah*
Haaah Hands... so sweaty.... Can buh *hah* *hah* barely hold the controller.
Hah So hot... take off my top, willya?
hah *hah* Hey! That's my rear you're attacking!
It's your own *hah* fault! You left yourself *hah* wiiiiiide open!
Luh-lay off, Marie! My ass can't take *hah* that hard a pounding!
Awww... *hah* *hah* Can't widdle Awex take the heat when a girl is dealing it? You never complain when you take it from *hah* *hah* guys!
...

Groan...
Grooooan...
You two look out of sorts.
Penelope, you have nooooo idea.
Yeah, we overexerted ourselves, no thanks to Marie.
You knew what you were getting into!
I didn't know you'd be getting that crazy with it! I'll be sore for days.
I told you they were doin' it.
But I hear Alex is into guys too.

So, Alex & Marie are doin' it huh? I wish she'd go out with me, she keeps turning me down.
I'd just like to go out with a girl and have it mean something for once.
Mnmm.
Maybe it won't last because Alex likes guys.
Gosh! Alex is gay... or bi, I guess? I mean, no big deal, but after you learn that about somebody, you can't help but think of him a little differently--
...Uh-oh.

Shower Thoughts

So... home sweet home, I guess.
Regrettably.
Couldn't you have picked someplace nicer?
I didn't know **I'd** be living here!
HA! You just wanted to make me suffer! Well, that **TOTALLY BACKFIRED!** Now you're the one stuck in this dump, and I'M...
HONK HONK
...
Furnishings are here.
<Sign here, please.>
<Oo! Can we convince you **big strong men** to carry our furniture to our room?>
<We would love to-->
<But a very striking woman gave us a generous tip, on the condition you do it yourselves.>
<She says it builds character!>

Lift with your knees, doorachka!
Shut up! I know what I'm doing!
Turn it towards you.
No, towards you.
The other "towards you!"
It's so heaaaaaaaavy! How many flights of stairs have we done?
Half a front stoop.
Moaaaaaaaaaan!

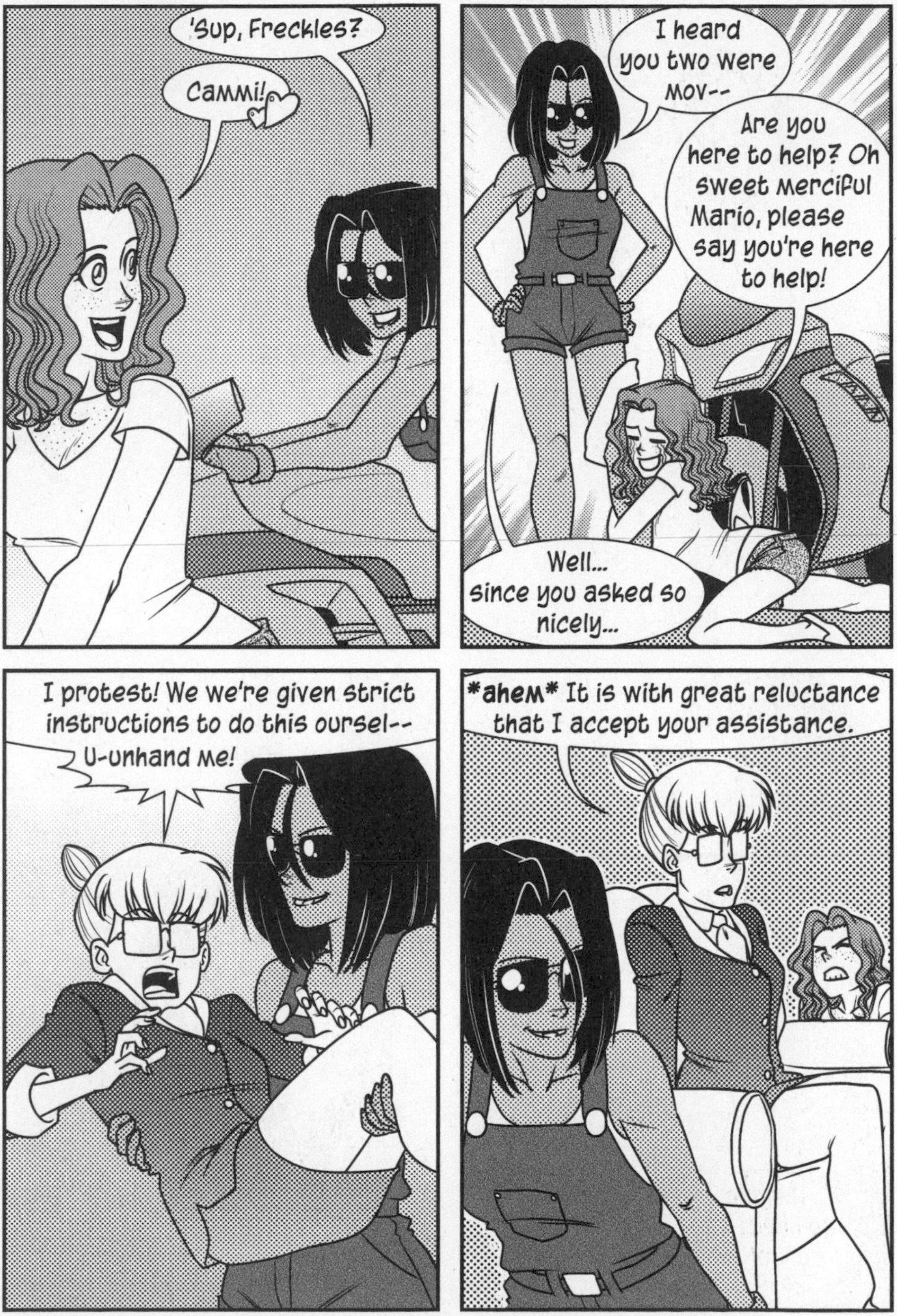
'Sup, Freckles?
Cammi!
I heard you two were mov--
Are you here to help? Oh sweet merciful Mario, please say you're here to help!
Well... since you asked so nicely...
I protest! We we're given strict instructions to do this oursel--
U-unhand me!
ahem It is with great reluctance that I accept your assistance.

Where shall I put these?
Gawd, Cammi! How do you do it? You're so strong!
Sure am! Bam! Feel this muscle.
That's amazing!
And my abs... don't forget my abs.
They're so tight! I'm so jealous of you.
I hope you're not expecting us to pay you a gratuity.
That's okay...
And this ass! My Gawd, I want this ass so bad!
It's been taken care of!

While "the help" assembles the bed frame, I believe it's time we address the elephant in the room.
Not Mr. Snoofles!
I refer to the fact that there are two of us and only one bedroom.
Well, the apartment was for me, so I get it, right?
I found the apartment, that room is my finder's fee. You can sleep on the couch!
As if! I should be th--
Bed is done!
BUNK BED!?
Around now, they'll be discovering the bunk bed...
Ah, life. It has its moments.

Cammi, I brought you some towels.
Thanks, Freckles. Put them next to my clothes, willya? That heavy lifting sure is sweaty work.
Oh, hey... It's your sunglasses. You know, I don't think I've ever seen you without them.
If you want to find out, you can hop in here with me.
Right! Like I'm **that** curious.
Suit yourself. You may never get a better chance, tho'.
Psst! Tatiana!
What is it now?
What do Cammi's eyes look like?
How should I know? She's always wearing those opaque glasses of hers.
Well, now I simply **have** to know!

Okay, I'm here, your eyes better sparkle like diamonds or shoot lasers.
Gosh... I... I didn't think you would take me up on that.
It's just... I don't let just anyone see me in this state.
God, I feel so vulnerable... nakeder than naked...
Cammi... you... don't have to--
!
Pfffft- HA HA HA HA! Oh Gawd, Freckles! Y-your face!
I couldn't h-help my she-ehl-ehlfffff AHA HA HA HA.....
...

You wear goggles in the shower?
A driver relies on her vision! Last thing you want is shampoo getting in there.
Protip: Also great for going down on guys, in case one pops early.
Gah! You gave me a Jimmy Tompson flashback!
Although you generally don't need them when going down on girls.
Man, I'm never gonna actually see your eyes, am I?
Well, maybe if you buy me a drink first.
Ha ha!
...
I don't get it...

Cammi, if I didn't know any better, I'd swear you were hitting on me.
Freckles, please! If I were hitting on you, I'd say something like...
I want to kiss all of your freckles one after the other.
Ha! It would take something like that for me to clue in, wouldn't it?
?
!!
Heyyyy.... look who crossed the finish line.

You mean you have a crush on M-- I am like, super naked right now, aren't I?
Guilty on both counts. Not a problem, is it?
A-are you kidding? Y-you're like the coolest person to ever say they like me.
B-but you should know... I've been down this road before. You know, being with a woman. And it didn't work out.
Why not?
Huh... you know I never really gave it much thought.
Well maybe you need to experiment a little more to figure that out.
!
You couldn't tell, but I was winking just now.

Exp-p-periment? Like... touching your skin?
If that's what you want, Freckles
It.... it is... what I... want...
WHO SAID THAT!?
I believe you did, Freckles.
BAD SANDRA!
Heh, you always were a grabby one. Maybe now we know why.
Well, help yourself, freckles, my cheeks are all yours.
You know... my ofver cheekfs are more fun.
THESE ARE FINE FOR NOW!

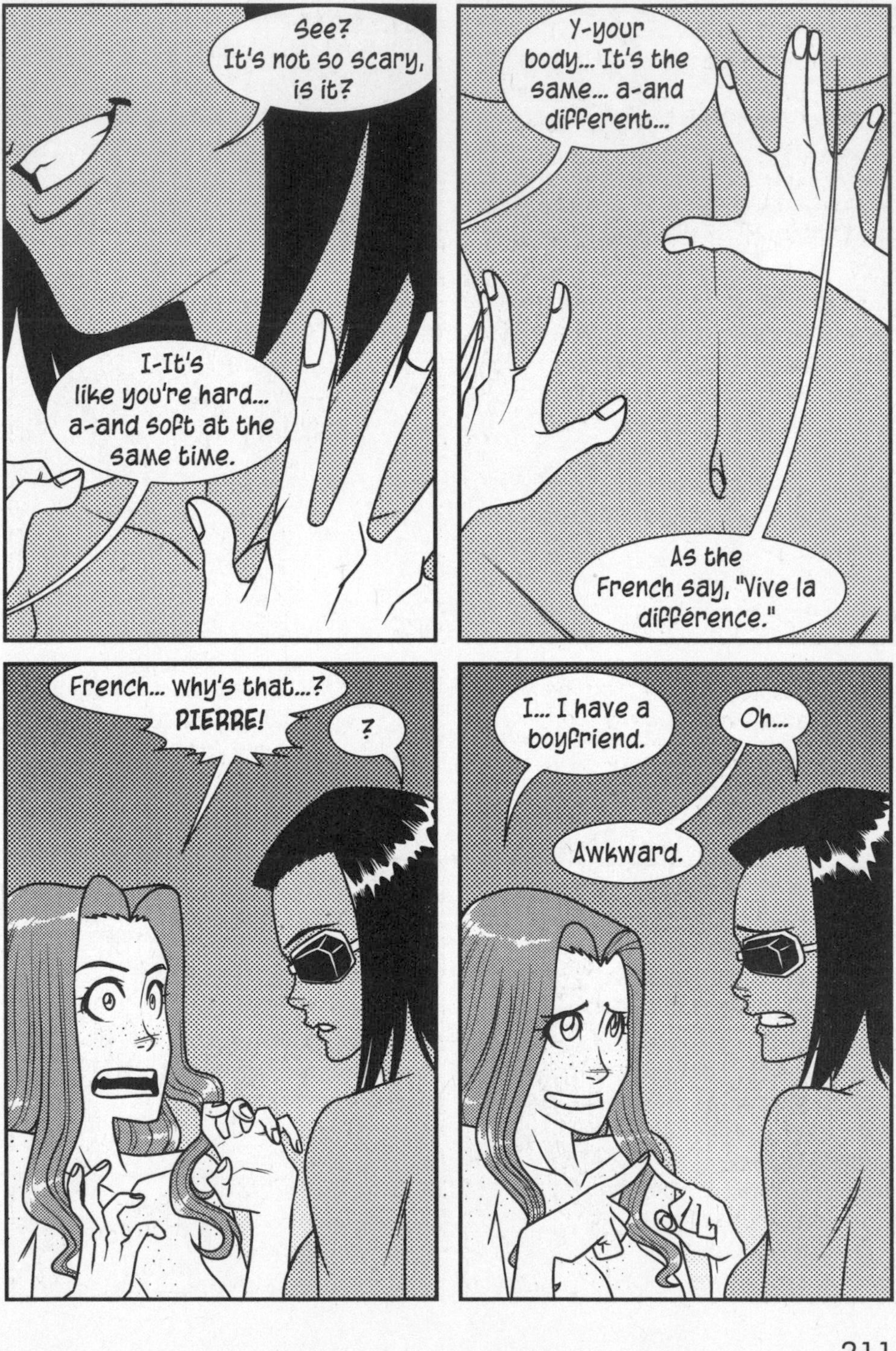
See? It's not so scary, is it?
I-It's like you're hard... a-and soft at the same time.
Y-your body... It's the same... a-and different...
As the French say, "Vive la différence."
French... why's that...? PIERRE!
?
I... I have a boyfriend.
Oh...
Awkward.

Ssso... boyfriend, huh?
Y-yeah.
Stupid, stupid!
Is it serious?
It's getting there.
Good looking, right?
Unf! To die for!
I-I mean... Cammi, I...
Don't sweat it, Freckles. Some things just can't be helped.
You coming out?
I-in a sec...
I-I just need one last blast of cold waAAAHH THAT'S COLD!
Heh. Still got it.

Thank you so much for all your help, Cammi. A-and I'm sorry about--
Don't worry about it. Doesn't mean we can't stay friends.
Sssso.... after all this... do I get to see your eyes?
Awwww.... Freckles...
!
SMECK!
Not a chance!
Meanie!

The Gamer Trio

C'est ça!
Casse-toi!
Avec plaisir!
Je ne veux plus jamais te voir!
Moi non plus!
Connasse!
Salope!
?
Is everything all--
Alehhhhhx!
Claire broke up with me-hee-hee-heeeeeeee......
GLOMP!
sniff ...
also, I'm gay.

Lavali, I could tell.
Y-you could? B-but I kept things so professional!
Really?
Aleeeeeeex! You're uh... up early... for once...
gooooooooood....
This is Claire!
Hi.
DARK MATTER GAMES
She, uh... slept over because we were up all night working on a project together.
I thought I knew everyone at DM Games.
Hm? I ahm an intérieur décoratisse. What makes you theenk I wourk at DM Gehmes?
Uh... your shirt?
Oh! Zis ees your sister's—
WHO WANTS WAFFLES?
DARK MATTER GAMES
TUNK!

Just promise me you won't tell Mum and Dad.
They know.
I just don't think they could handle my being gay.
Lavali, they know.
I admit there were some close calls, but I always covered them up.
We... We were practicing skinny dipping! F-for our camping trip!
Sh-she's having chest pains! I'm giving her CPR!
Suh-Silvie's learning to be a gynecologist! I... I'm helping her with her homework!

Wh-what are you--
It's an awkward sibling hug, just let it happen.
Listen, you know I love you... but you were terrible at keeping that secret... just... just the worst.
Honestly, I don't think anyone close to you didn't know.
Oh, dear. I see tears. Is everything all right?
Get this: Lavali thought people didn't know she was gay.
YOU'RE GAY!?
I mean... yeah! Of course I knew... This doesn't change my worldview at all...
Does Claire know?

Lavali's gay? I... I had no idea...
I get this doesn't change anything, but it's just... she hid it so well!
Wait! Could it run in the family? Could Alex be gay too?
C'mere, Nathan Drake, it's time you discovered my uncharted treasure.
Mmmmmmaybe I could deal with that.

Snnnnnzzxxxsss....
Bozhe moi! I did not think it possible, but she is even more annoying asleep than awake!
I might as well get up and--
WHAP!
Znxx-hm?
Do try and be careful, dorogáya. You know how clumsy you can be.
Hnnngh!

Oof! What a way to start my day off.
Bah! Days off are for the weak.
I will spend my day contributing to society.
Hey! I'll have you know I'll be spending my day bettering myself as a model!
I'll be meeting my new "consultant," who will be putting me on a strict regimen of movies, comic books, and video games.
Strict, eh?
...
I'll leave you to your grueling labors, then.

Okay... I'm going to meet Sandra. No big, right? Right? Is it warm in here? What if she doesn't like the coffee here?
Keep it together. Alex. Just be suave. Girls dig that, right? Just pull out her chair, and compliment her looks...
Or do I compliment and then pull out? M-maybe I should call Marie--
...
AHH! How long have you been sitting there!?
I dunno, three minutes?

Ha-have you been playing the games like I a-asked!
I've been playing my Weeyoo every chance I get, not that I get much time to myself.
Not to mention how tired I am sometimes. Posing in lingerie all day can be exhausting.
Luh-luh--
Mmm... Up, up, down, down, baby!
I know it's hard to imagine, but...
Alex?

Ah! Y-yes! That's good for gaming at home, b-but what about when you're on the go?
I can't play my Weeyoo outside!
The gamepad loses its signal when I leave the apartment.
I've tried!
Well, not your home console. What about your portable system? You know, for on the subway, o-or between breaks?
Oh! Like a Game Boy? I don't have one of those.
Y-you don't?
Should I?
TAKE MINE!
?

Y-you're giving this... to me?
Sure! They send me tons for review purposes!
I have a drawer full! No big deal! It's not like it's a rare special edition!
Oh cute! It has a Carmen Chamelia on the cover.
Ahh! That IS a rare special edition!
Marie's gonna kill me!
You're sweet. Thanks.
!
SO WORTH IT!
?

So, teacher... what's on the curriculum today?
H-how 'bout a movie?
I'd love to... but my entertainment budget has sort of been slashed recently and...
I... I'll pay!
Oo... I couldn't...
I insist! It's important you stay current with pop culture.
But...
Teacher's orders!
It's a date, then.
A Duh-duh-duh-daaaaaate?

That was fun. What did you think of the movie?
What movie?

You've never played a Zelda game?
No, should I have?
Yes! Let me get you one!
Let's see... I think Ocarina of Time to start...
sob sob
?
What's wrong with your sister?
Don't worry about it, she just got dumped by her girlfriend.
Ohhhh...
You're gay?
?

I mean... oh nooooo.... You had your heart broken? C'mere!
SNIFF Sandra, I didn't hear you come in... I'm sorry. I must look a mess.
Don't worry about that, silly.
And yeah... I-I'm gay...
God! It feels so good to say that out loud!
Well, I had no idea. Seriously you were so good at hiding it. Like some kind of lesbian ninja.
Aww... that's sweet of you to say.
Told you.

Right! We need to get you right back on that horse again! We're going cruising for girls!
!!
Wha--?
Hmm... now what could we wear?
Suh-suh-Sandra! W-we can't go out c-cruising just like that!
Huh... you're right. I mean, what would my boyfriend say..?
Aw, he'll be fine. It's not like I'm going cruising for guys!

Here we are.
"Omoikane." I've never heard of it... Must be trendy.
Oh, it is! I called Cammi and asked her for the trendiest gay bar in Paris.
Um... Did you specify you wanted a lesbian bar?
No... why?

BRRRRN!
BRRRRN!
Go away.
Éva, darling, you'll never guess who just walked into "Omoikane's."
I swear to god Lukas, if this is about the size of your table's "dragon roll" again...
Perhaps I should send you a picture.
!!
Find out what she wants!
I've got you this time, Zoé!

What kind of place is this?
OMG! They serve sushi on naked men? That is literally two of my favorite things!
Ladies! It is so rare to see such ravishing creatures grace this establishment.
Other than myself, naturally.
Please! I insist that you join me.
Can we?
No!
But he INSISTS!
In what UNIVERSE would this be "cruising for gir--"
PLEEEEEEASE?

Awwww... okay, okay...
I'm sorry, uh...
Lukas.
We can't take you up on your offer. We need to find a lesbian bar.
Lesbian bar?
Yes, I'm trying to get Lavali here dating again. Do you know of any?
Allow me to ask Siri.
"Siri," darling, did you get all of that?
Yes... Send them to Natacha's. I'll meet you there.
I found just the place, come! I will escort you!
Um... Won't they object to you?
Darling, please! No woman is that gay.

Ladies, I trust this is more to your liking?
I... I think I was less nervous when it was just men!
Don't say that! You'll do fine, I know it.
See? You're turning heads already, you seductress, you.
<Hi, gorgeous. Buy you a drink?>

<My name's Anette, what's yours?>
S-Sandra... but this is Lavali.
Pleasure.
Lavali's a production assistant at Dark Matter Games. She knows the gaming business like the back of her hand!
Hm... And what do you do?
Who me? Pfft! Nothing special really, I'm just a boring ol' model.
A model, you say? Come! You MUST meet my friends!

Not enjoying yourself, darling?
Humph! Story of my life! I go to a lesbian bar and my straight friend gets all the attention.
Still... I'd still be crying at home if it wasn't for Sandra.
No way I'd have had the nerve to go clubbing on my own.
Oh, well. I may as well go save her.
Woo hoo! Lesbians are aw'sum! *hic*

Sandra... What are you doing?
Havi'n fuuuuuuun! *hic*
Do I need to remind you're not the lesbian?
hic Don' choo tell me what I'm not. I'll tell me to tell you to tell me what I'm not!
Wait... who's doing what now?
Omigosh! You've got one of those whatchacallits... "bindis?"
Yes, I wear it to be closer to my heritage. I'm a very spiritual person, you know?
They say the bindi can reveal my soul.
Huh... Iss not working for me...
!!
?

Sandra! That was very, very culturally insensitive!
Wasn't it?
Eh... L'il bit...
Bu'... But Lavaliiiiii...
I'm sorry... Your name is Lavali?
sigh... Yes... My parents went through a hippie phase.
They sure got out of it in time for my brother to be born, though.
I... I'm sorry, It's a lovely name. I just never heard a Sanskrit name for someone so.. so...
Alabaster?
Lets go with that.
You two should talk.
Sandra!
And don' worry, Aaina! Once ya get t' know her, Lavali isn' an alabastard at all!

And then she says "No... but I've got crabbies!"
Ha ha ha! That's so funny, Lavali.
Sandra was right, meeting new people was just what I needed.
I like taking to you, Lavali, I feel like I can open up to you about anything.
B-BUMP! B-BUMP!
Not at all like when I'm attracted to someone. When that happens, I get all shaky and nervous.
Oh...?
So do you know if Sandra has a girlfriend?
I sort of have a crush on her.

Y-you like Sandra?
MM-hmm! I mean, Anette is coming on strong, but I think I have a chance.
Well, I hate to break it to you, but the truth about Sandra is that she's--
She's...
The truth is, I know for a fact that she does not have a girlfriend.
Aa! You've made my day, Lavali!
LESBEANS RUUUUULE!

You know, I've been meaning to become more sexually adventurous. I just had my spare room remodeled into... a sex dungeon.
Why don't you and I break it in by--
whisper whisper whisper.
Heeee...
Whisper whisper badminton racket, whisper whisper plastic tube whisper whisper Mexican ghost peppers.
...
I want to go home.
Now? But we--
I'm not as adventurous as I thought!

Where is she?
Here to destroy her so soon? Pity. I found her quite entertaining.
Oh my sweet beautiful man-slave, you always did lack imagination.
Why destroy her, when I can use her as my catspaw to destroy Zoé?
Ambitious.
Yes, I'm rather proud of it.
I do however take offense to your earlier statement. I have a rather vivid imagination.
In fact, I'm imagining what Zoé will do to you if she finds you sniffing around her protégé, right now.
!!

Damn you, Lukas, your logic is as rock solid as your abs.
Still if it's insider information on Zoé you're after...
Might I suggest going through a third party?
The friend?
Yes, they appear quite close, I'd wager she tells her everything.
Innnteresting...
Lukas, I do believe it is time I embraced the love that dare not speak its name.
You? Good heavens! I'd better send a letter of condolence to every male in Paris.

Omigawwwd! Underbewwwwb! I'mma sqweeeeeze it!
Sandra, no! If you have to squeeze someone's breasts then.. then... squeeze mine!
What a night... It's like babysitting a ten year old. A horny, mammary-obsessed--
It's exactly like babysitting a ten year old.
Uh...
I... I HAVE NEVER SEEN THIS WOMAN GROPING ME BEFORE IN MY LIFE!
Squishyyyyy...

Shoo! Go grope someone else!
Heee...
H-hi... My name's Lovely-- LAVALI--
I couldn't help but notice you staring at me...
W-with your eyes... You have... two... They're lovely.
And now you're scribbling on my hand... A-and I'm okay with that!
Ohh.. It's a phone number! I love phone numbers! They're wonderful!
J-just the best!
Whose is it?

S-so.. you don't talk much, do you? T-talking is overrated anyways. I-I don't talk much mys--
Meep
Call me.
squeak
EXCUSE ME. Does this belong to you?
Don't even care.
Underbewwwwwwwwbs!

Wheeee! T'nite was th'best!
Sure was!... Uh... let me go write something down real quick.
I could've sworn I parked my car around here s'mwhere?
You don't have a car, Sandra. And you're in no shape to go home tonight.
You're sleeping here, I insist! I'll sleep on the sofa. You can have my room, in the--
I can find it! I'm not that drunk, y'know?
Z!
...

Is- is this for real? is this really happening? Is Sandra r-really in m-my bed?
Z!
She's so close and so warm... Is this... Is this what Heaven feels like?
Hi, lover, I hope you don't mind my sneaking into your room? I just have one teensy question for you.
Mhm?
What are all these pictures of me doing on your wall, you creepo?
!!
I'm so dead!

Ohh.. my head... How much did I drink last night?
OMIGOSH! This must be Alex's room.
Wait... This doesn't look like Lavali's room...?
Thank heavens he wasn't there, or I'd have died from embarrassment!
I wonder where he went?
B-BUMP
B-BUMP
B-BUMP

Sandra?
Oh, hey, Marie.
What are you doing here so early?
Spent the night. Lavali and I went out and, well, one thing led to another.
Anyways, busy day today, talk to you later, kay?
One thing? WHAT thing? And what's the OTHER thing?
- + = ...
WE'RE LESBIANS!
!

PUFF!
Ha ha! I... I'M jumping to conclusions... I must be, right?
Marie! Thank heavens you're here! I need to talk to someone... woman to woman.
Omigosh, you consider me an equal? I feel so levelled up!
Okay, so... after experiencing an intimate, intense moment with someone... how long before you should call them back?
!
LESBIANS AGAIN!

Sandra's a lesbian, Lavali's a lesbian... It's like every woman I know is now a lesbian.
Wait... Am I a lesbian?
Hey... yeah! I should be a lesbian! I would have SO much in common with Sandra. We'd be gay BFF's!
That's the best kind of BFF!
All right! Starting today, I'll be into girls! A brand new outlook on li--
Aaa! Nintendo sent me a review copy of the new Zelda game! I have to play this right now!
Unf! Link, come to Momma!

GOAAAAAAAAAL!
TILLEUX
He did it! He did it! Christophe won the game!
Would it kill you two to pay a little more attention?
We are paying attention!
This boss is really hard!

Congratulations, Christophe!
Thanks Penelope.
Ew! You're all sweaty and smelly.
You love it.
Hey there, football star. I suppose you'll have a victory party to go to.
Aw, you know I'd rather hang with you guys.
We really are all proud of you, Christophe.
Proud enough to go out on a date with me?
HA HA! Oh Christophe, you're such a joker! We can't ALL go on a date with you!

Just one date, Marie! What can it hurt?
Christophe, we've been over this before! We're too good friends!
And I don't want to mess up our group.
...just to become another notch on your bedpost.
No... you don't understand! It's because we're such good friends that I want to go out with you.
The other girls... they just throw themselves at me. I.. I'm looking for something more...
Though maybe it's something you already have with Alex.
Ha ha! Us? Have a thing? Th-that's crazy! You're crazy! Did Penelope just call me? I... I'd better go check! Craaaazy Christophe!
Those two are so doing it.

Hey, lover...
Marie? Wh-what ar--
I've had a change of heart, but on one condition...
It has to be both of us.
Oh, boy... Fantasy-Me was way too okay with that idea.

Forget about the future, Christophe. Focus on having fun.
Yeah, forget about how you got turned down by the only girl you have a meaningful connection with.
Forget the hollow feeling you get from meaningless sex with all those other girls.
Okay... I'll admit that last one is a little hard to ignore at the moment.
Oh Christoffffffff!

The problem is that the girls, everyone on the team... they don't like me... They like the idea of me.
The big man on campus, Mr. Invincible Football Star. But I don't think I've ever been happier than when I used to play video games with Alex and Marie.
Hey, what do you think of video games?
Uhhh, isn't that kid stuff? I think only creepy looo-zers play those. LOL!
Mmm.
Christophe?
I heard you guys were short a creepy loser?
Come in, Penelope snuck us some hard lemonade and we're about to play dumb campfire games.
See? Now that's fun!

Sweet dreams.
Written by Dave Lumsdon
Drawn by Eisu
... you did a passable job today. By your standards, that's an improvement.
Hooray for me. Can we go now?
Not now. I need to talk business with the producer.
But my feet are killing meeeee...
Go wait in the limo!
Tell ME to go to the limo... grumble... I'll tell HER to go to the limo!
Tough day at the office, Freckles?
Just Zoé being Zoé.
Ha! Been there, bought the T-shirt.
Hey, sorry for making things awkward the other day...
HM? When was that?

You know... In the shower.
I... I wouldn't say it was "awkward"..... I mean... you really got in touch with a part of me, y'know? Besides, ever since that day I've been having... well, erotic dreams.
Uhhh... Good for you!
A... about you...
!
I... I can't believe I just said that out loud!
Well I hope Fantasy Me lives up to the real thing.
It wasn't like thaaaaat...
You see... In my dream I'm sunbathing... nude...
I like it already!

On your ass...
Come again?
In my dream, You're a giant, and I'm on your ass and... I love it.
You getting enough light, freckles?
Mmm... I could stay here allll day!
Cute.
I know... I I know... I'm so weird!
No... I'm flattered, really...
At least you have your boyfriend's buns to console you.
Yeah... I know, I have a boyfriend. But sometimes, when I think of that day with you and me in the shower...
...I wish I didn't.
...
...
Mff mff MFF mff

One... Kiss
Two... Kiss
Three... Kiss
Mmm... Kiss my freckles! Kiss ALL of my freckles!
!
Ah..... N-now you know my secret!
You see... I was born with Girly anime eyes...
What?
Now you know why I wore those dark glasses.
WHAT!?

Now my mystique of a cool driver is ruined!
Wait... Is this a dream?
Am I having another erotic dream?
I don't believe it... I finally admit all of that and it was a dream? It was all for nothing?
Well I wouldn't say "nothing..."
You see... you fell asleep in the limo...
Huh?
And you talk in your sleep.
Wh--
Mmm... Cammi...
Cammmmmmi!
Yup! Cammi's still got a shot!
Spank me harder!

Sandra's escapades continue NEXT VOLUME!

SANDRA ON THE ROCKS Volume 2

ISBN: 978-1-77294-124-1

In stores MAY 2020!

The fabulous Dillon in his own MA3 spin-off!

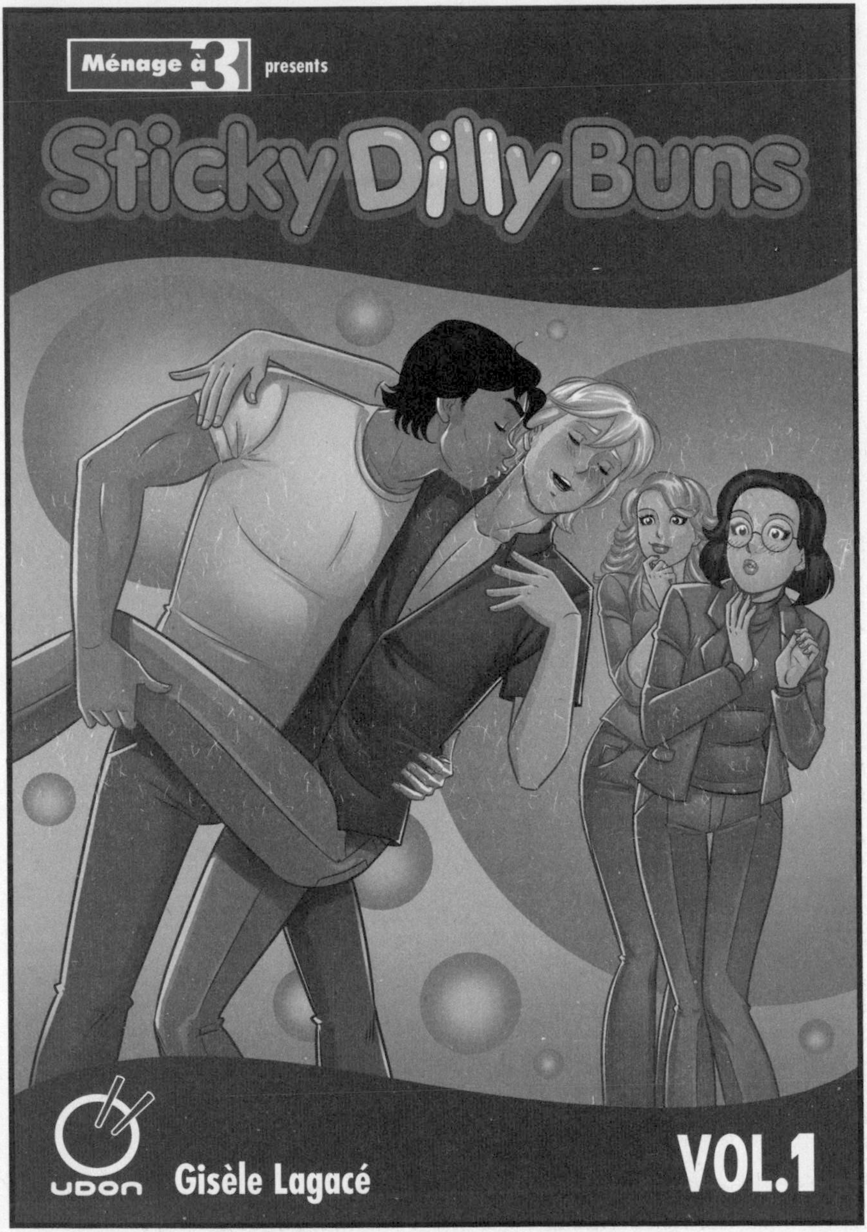

STICKY DILLY BUNS Volume 1

ISBN: 978-1-77294-121-0

In stores FEBRUARY 2020!

See Sandra's sexy orgins in MÉNAGE À 3!

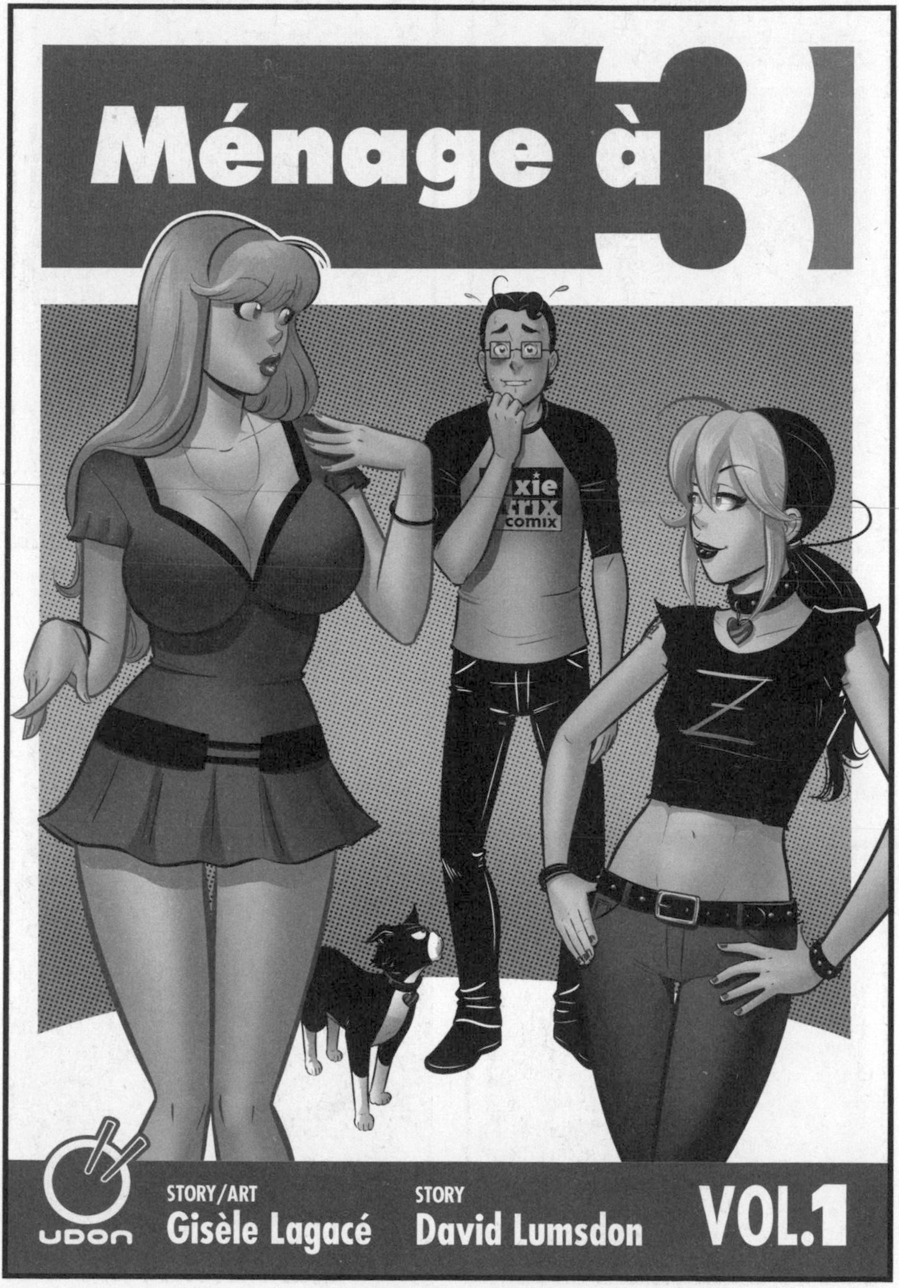

MÉNAGE À 3 Volume 1

ISBN: 978-1-77294-059-6

MÉNAGE À 3 Volume 2

ISBN: 978-1-77294-066-4

MÉNAGE À 3 Volume 3

ISBN: 978-1-77294-090-9

MÉNAGE À 3 Volume 4

ISBN: 978-1-77294-106-7

MÉNAGE À 3 Volume 5

ISBN: 978-1-77294-123-4

PERSONA 3 VOL.1
ISBN-13: 978-1927925850

PERSONA 4 VOL.1
ISBN-13: 978-1927925577

STRAVAGANZA VOL.1
ISBN-13: 978-1772941036

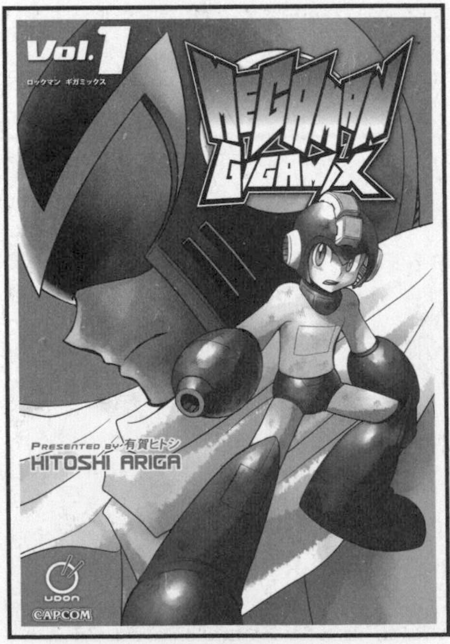

MEGA MAN GIGAMIX VOL.1
ISBN-13: 978-1926778235

Sandra ON THE ROCKS

VOLUME 1
OMNIBUS

Story: DAVID LUMSDON
Art/Lettering: SAIFUL REMY "EISU" MOKHTAR
Series Editor: T CAMPBELL

UDON STAFF
Chief of Operations: ERIK KO
Director of Publishing: MATT MOYLAN
VP of Business Development: CORY CASONI
Director of Marketing: MEGAN MAIDEN
Japanese Liaisons: STEVEN CUMMINGS
ANNA KAWASHIMA

SANDRA ON THE ROCKS: VOLUME 1 OMNIBUS

Published by UDON Entertainment Inc.
118 Tower Hill Road, C1, PO Box 20008
Richmond Hill, Ontario, L4K 0K0 CANADA

www.UDONentertainment.com

First Printing: October 2019
ISBN-13: 978-1772941135
ISBN-10: 1772941131

Printed in Canada